Born Beneath a Rainbow

Born Beneath a Rainbow

Memories of a Country Childhood

Judith Ellmers

NEW WOMEN'S PRESS
Auckland

To my parents, the late Ivy Emma
and Alick McGregor Trafford

© Judith Ellmers 1983
First published 1983

ISBN 0 908652 02 X

Photoset in Goudy
by Jacobson Typesetters Ltd, Auckland
and printed by
Whitcoulls Ltd, Christchurch

Published by New Women's Press Ltd,
P.O. Box 47-339, Auckland

Contents

1 The Valley Farm 7

2 Grandma's Cottage 9

3 Early Life at Home 18

4 The Roadmaking 29

5 School 37

6 Holidays on the Flats 45

7 Summer 52

8 The Depression 56

9 Milestones 64

10 Growing Up 69

11 Explorations 75

12 Neighbours and Legends 80

13 Better Times 86

14 Grandmother 90

15 Beyond the Gorge 92

16 Epilogue 98

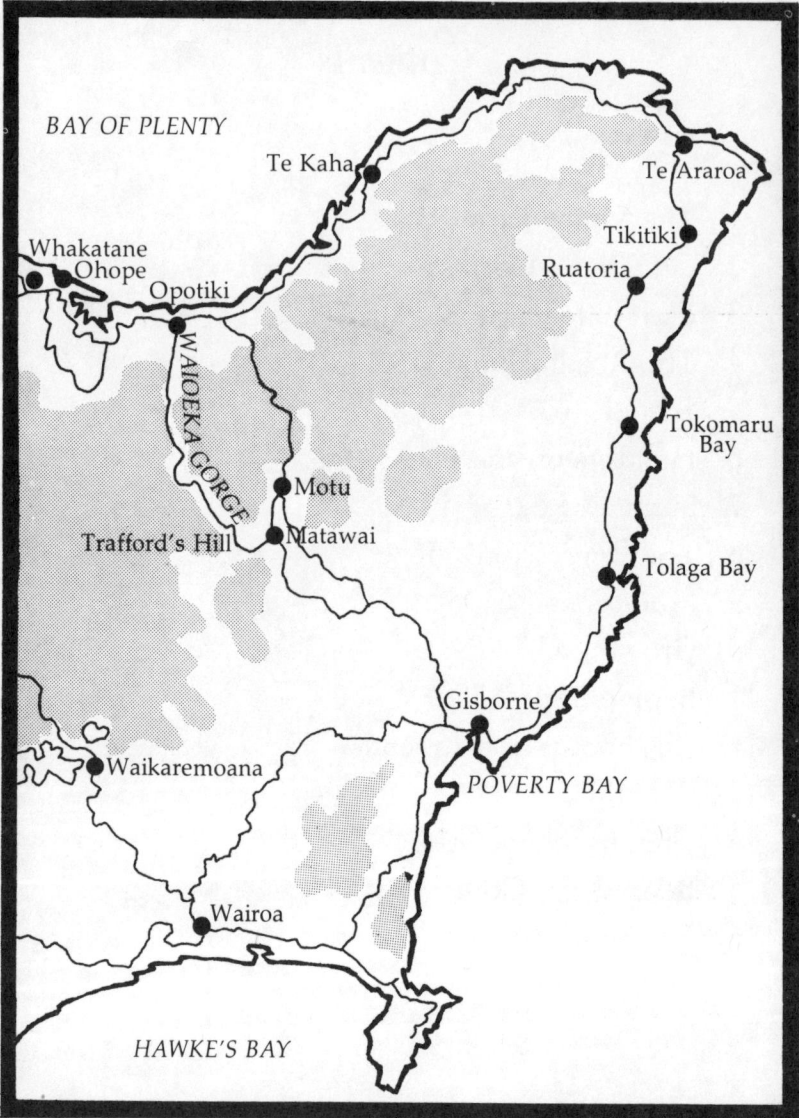

BAY OF PLENTY

Te Kaha

Te Araroa

Tikitiki

Ruatoria

Whakatane
Ohope

Opotiki

WAIOEKA GORGE

Motu

Trafford's Hill

Matawai

Tokomaru
Bay

Tolaga Bay

Gisborne

POVERTY BAY

Waikaremoana

Wairoa

HAWKE'S BAY

Drawn by Lyndy McIntyre

1

The Valley Farm

At the homestead my father sat upon the sturdy steps of the open porch, purposefully lacing his boots, tying the leather thongs firmly around his ankles for support, in preparation for many hours of walking. He was about to muster 'the tops' of the hill farm, an operation which was always carried out on foot. Larry, my brother, and I, four and five years old respectively, watched him enviously.

'Where are you going today, Dad?'

'The Top Burn,' he said abruptly. 'Too far for you kids. But you might meet me at the top gate later on. You'll hear the dogs.'

'Ooh, can we, can we?' was the joyous response. We planned rapidly — we could eel along the creek, then follow the new fence line to the tawa bush. The shiny purple tawa berries would be plump and firm, each with a sticky nut in the centre. They were satisfying to the touch but we had found long ago that they had an acrid flavour. Anyway, we could collect a kit full of them for the household pigs.

And so we would come to the top gate on the high cleared ridge overlooking the homestead, there to await the shouts, barking and bleating, heralding the arrival of the mob of sheep. Then we would walk with father driving the sheep to the woolshed yards. . . .

But aromas of porridge, bacon and eggs, and golden crisp fried bread, all cooking on the black range with its fire in the wood-burner open for warmth, turned our thoughts to breakfast. Mother was calling us. Father had long since completed his.

Pale early morning sunlight lay across the very tops of the hills making them seem luminous, desirable, mysterious. But the farm house and garden, still shrouded in frost, were cold and blue-shadowed in the valley bottom. Soon, though, we would have our boots on and be climbing to the exciting eminence of the top gate.

From our first consciousness, the tops and what lay beyond were

a challenge to us. We longed to go up to that horizon so far above
our abode, where the fence posts and gates were stark black in the
white light of dawn and twilight, and a burnt tree stump, a horse
or a cow might be silhouetted entrancingly. Up there and beyond,
we thought, was The World — more hills and mountains, bush,
rivers, towns and the sea.

For the homestead was enclosed by the hills in a unique way. It
stood amidst its English trees — oaks, pines and poplars — on the
narrow valley bottom. The bush-covered hills about us formed the
sides of a deep mountain bowl situated at the head of the Waioeka
Gorge, between Gisborne and Opotiki on the east coast of the
North Island. Many creeks converge to form the main stream, the
Waioeka. The surrounding peaks are part of the Raukumara range,
a tumbled mass of mountains heaped skywards and sharply
ravined. They form a continuation of the central spine of Maui's
'fish' of Maori legends about the genesis of the North Island.

Our farm lay in the fastnesses of these ranges, and about ninety-
seven kilometres north-west of Gisborne, the coastal city of Poverty Bay. Much of this country is still clothed in the original beech
rain forest which grows luxuriantly in the shallow layer of sandy
loam covering the granite-like rock. To the west it merges with the
vast central forest of the North Island, the Urewera.

According to our other cultural heritage, Waioeka is more than
a little like parts of Scotland, perhaps another ' . . . Caledonia stern
and wild. Meet nurse for a poetic child . . . ' Anyway, such vivid
concepts of mountain country as those of Scott and Edvard Grieg,
made an immediate impact upon us when we came upon them in
our reading and listening. We, too, passionately loved our environment with its riches of forest, clear streams and lofty mountains
with their abrupt changes of mood.

Forty or so years ago, in my early childhood, the road north from
Gisborne had not penetrated far into these mountains and stopped
short of 'the Hill', 700 metres high and part of the main range. Just
over the Hill lay the farm. It was not until the late nineteen twenties that the road was continued on to Opotiki, the township
situated on the Bay of Plenty coast. And so we children grew up in
this remote spot completely enclosed by mountains. For the most
part we were happy living the life of the bush.

2

Grandma's Cottage

My earliest explorations took me crawling, slowly and at times painfully, past the pungent lacebarks, past the woodheap with the fascinating pale orange matai sawdust and cleanly splintered chips, past the men's whare with its masculine smells of rank tobacco and carbolic soap wafting from the open door, and on to Grandma's cottage, where dwelt delight in many forms.

Often one of our lively young aunts would be staying with Grandma, on holiday from teaching or nursing. Aunt Nan might bring out the golden syrup tin and a slab of home-baked bread. 'Our dear little Beetle,' she would say. 'Fancy coming all this way by yourself!' Then she would wash my hands and face, and there would be much kissing and encouragement. Grandmother, too, would praise this feat after making some dismayed exclamations at the state of my clothing. Then Aunt Nan would show me the rag book of trains, depicting improbably snorting black locomotives from other countries. I especially remember the one from Mexico with a great spiny cactus in the picture which I somehow connected with the splinters of the chipheap. To enjoy the train and Grandma's company I had to brave the splinters, just as the Mexican explorers braved the spiny cactus. I learnt early that achievement has its hard side, a necessary lesson for our kind of life.

Grandmother was of Scottish family. She was a cultured woman, upright in gait and character. But she had the kindest of hearts and often betrayed her sterner principles where her grandchildren were concerned, especially the very young ones. She was a spare slender woman, with a rather formal manner, and piercing blue eyes which missed nothing. Her fine snowy hair was dressed meticulously in a neat bun, and her high-necked dresses and white aprons always seemed to be spotless. Grandfather, a quiet steadfast man, had died suddenly of a heart attack. She never spoke of him — perhaps the grief was very deep.

Grandmother's father was a direct descendant of Corrychoillie, chief of the Clan Cameron. Great Grandfather had received training for the British diplomatic service and as a young girl Grandmother must have absorbed much of the social formality pertaining to this background. But the family had come to New Zealand, first to Southland and then to Poverty Bay. Grandmother was married from one of the pioneer homesteads on 'the flats', the home of her brother who had founded a prosperous farm on the fertile river plain of Gisborne. The two-storeyed home with its fine garden formed a dignified setting for the wedding and the gathering of many relatives. The family piper lifted the hearts of the kinsfolk with his skirling on ancient bagpipes which had once echoed in the glens of Scotland. Grandmother wore the Clan Cameron wedding veil of fine Irish lace. Two generations later, I, too, was to wear it, as did many other descendants. She was destined to live in the mountains, as she and her husband lived first at Wharerata and eventually settled in the mountainous Waioeka country.

When their sons were nearing adulthood they took up this rough block, mostly in standing bush. Somehow, while the felling and burning of the bush proceeded, they managed to wrest a living from it. No big mortgage for them — it was against Grandmother's principles, even if they had been able to raise such a commodity. The help of their sons was all-important in the venture, as they provided much of the hard labour required to pasture the land and earned money by working for other farmers. Extracts from a diary kept by Raymond, the younger son, as a lad of about 18 years, give a vivid picture:

1st Jan, 1913 *Papa sold some skins to — at 3/6 each.*
9th Jan, 1913 *Harvesting for Uncle [on flats] and threshing ryegrass for Mr. Newman at Kaiteratahi.*
Monday 20th Jan. *Burning part of the bush in our section. Also cutting tracks.*
Saturday 25th Jan. *Sowing grass seed and logging up on the flat.*
Sunday Feb. 2nd. *I put up a fly tent near the Rough Burn.*
Friday 7th March. *Put in a full day at the whare. As the timber wasn't splitting too well, we decided to build it of iron.*

8th Mar. *Papa went out to Mr. Buscke's [a neighbour ten kilometres over
'the Hill'] to ring up Common Shelton & Co. [a stock and station firm
in Gisborne] for the iron. [The iron would come by train, then by pack-
horse the last forty-eight kilometres.]*
Friday 21st *A very hot day. Splitting, lining and flooring for the 'whare'.*
Monday 24th *Hot day. Falling trees around homestead site. Papa making stretcher beds. [Made of pieces of four by two timber bolted together
and slung with sacking.] Mr. Brown stayed, and took ill. Charlie went
to neighbour's to fetch eggs for him. [An eight-kilometre ride for Charlie,
a younger son.] Papa went to Gisborne [Grandmother was staying with
her folk on the flats while the whare was made ready. 'Papa' would have
ridden forty-eight kilometres to Otoko, and taken the train from there to
Gisborne.]*
April 8th *Wet and showery day. Finished putting iron on the whare and
shifted into it, from the old tent.*
Tuesday 22nd. *Lovely day. Clearing the fence line. [around the new
dwelling] and digging strainer holes. Papa laid up with a bad back.*
23rd. *Charlie and I fencing. Alick [my father] nailing palings on the
walls and preparing Mama's room for her.*
24th. *Papa went out to Mr. Buscke's to get Mama. [She had stayed the
night en route.]*
25th. *Lovely day. Alick went to Matawai and brought two loads of stores
out.*

They had Mama, and the terrific moral support afforded by her
personality — and good food! And so the falling and logging up
went on until they had cleared 124 hectares (300 acres). But a dark
shadow was looming.

Sunday 27th April. *Showery day. Charlie and I left for Gisborne with
Eva. [Their sister.] Charlie and I went out to see the British warship lying
at anchor in the Bay, in the Gosford. [A lighter belonging to the port of
Gisborne.]*
Thursday Dec. 25th 1913 *Spent Xmas day at Toroa [One of the well
established family homes on the flats.] In the afternoon Mr. Thomas tried
to take the family photograph.*

That was Ray's last diary entry as a young farm lad. And it was the last photograph of the family all together. In due course, cheer-ful young Ray and Alick (my father) enlisted, and in 1918 only father came back. Ray had died of shell-shock in France.

His death was a bitter blow to the family, as a letter from Mama to her remaining Alick portrays. Written in her meticulous upright copper-plate it runs:

Waioeka,
Matawai.
Jan 2, 1918.

My dear Alick,

It seems so strange to have passed into a new year and to leave the old one with all its sadness for so many, and for me personally, it has been the darkest and heaviest of my life-time because of the many shocks I received. First Charlie's accident, which I almost witnessed, and then two months afterwards Eva's fall from her horse. She had slight concussion of the brain. I nursed and attended her without a nurse or Doctor. The latter, when he saw Eva, said that I had done the right thing. Charlie then arrived home very lame after six months away with his leg injury; then the news that my poor Boy was killed. It has been a shadowed year, but I thank God throughout it I have been kept by the Power of our Heavenly Father through a testing time which comes to all sooner or later. I am constantly thinking, thinking, of you my dear Boy safe in Hospital. Such a relief, but my thoughts wander back to the 'Trenches' where many old and new Boys are still fighting on. Oh, that it was over. I dreaded the winter for you Boys and neither of you are there . . . .

(My father was wounded and hospitalized in England at this time.)

Ray's death was especially hard for my father, who had been very attached to his younger brother and happy in his life in the hills until the tragedy of war overtook the family. Father, veteran of Ypres and Passchendaele, was, they said, much quieter and sterner after his return.

The Waioeka farm was now constituted as part of the soldier settlement of the Gorge country. It was named 'Raysburn' after the boy who never returned. John McCrae's poem 'In Flanders Fields', held special meaning for Father:

> 'If ye break faith with us who die,
> We shall not sleep, though poppies grow
> In Flanders fields.'

Upon his return to civilian life, like many another, he quietly accepted the challenge of doing the best one could in adverse circumstances; 'taking up the torch' and in this case, not turning from the struggle to bring into productivity land which was basically unsuitable for farming because of its steepness and inaccessibility.

After the war, Father married a bride who, like his mother, came from the foothill country nearer Gisborne. They settled first in the whare, and soon in a new house, just a stone's throw away. Grandmother remained in the whare which she called a cottage. Our home was a modern five-roomed house with attractive casement windows and wide porches. The material for it, and for Grandmother's cottage, had been packed in by horse teams from the end of the road which by now extended to the Gisborne side of 'the Hill'. The couple's first surviving child, for they lost their first-born, was similarly packed in, but in adverse circumstances. The dress-basket with the baby in it was firmly strapped mid-packsaddle and the horse swam safely over the dreaded Motu river crossing.

The child in the dress-basket happened to be me. As I was the eldest, my second name had been firmly decided upon: Corrychoillie, after the Clan Chief. (As a girl I hated the name, until I reached adulthood and learned its proud history.) Three more children followed in quick succession, and we soon became a close-knit family. Each was christened and godparented while still new infants, and before we were brought home into the mountains — at Grandmother's stern insistence no doubt.

Grandma and the aunts played a large part in our early experience. Their tawa-slab cottage had weathered to a pleasant dull silver and the iron was painted a brown red. In summer the cottage nestled snugly in its surrounding beds of day lilies, single red and yellow dahlias, pansies and old-fashioned sweet-william. A pillow shape of concrete formed by a sack of cement which had set in the damp was the front doorstep, for nothing was ever wasted! Deep-scented cabbage-roses grew everywhere, transplanted in cuttings from the former Southland home. Ivy completely covered the broad corrugated iron chimney piece as well as the nearby dairy, which, in summer heat, was a cool haven wreathed in greenery.

'Rough it', the family had to 'but let it be with as much grace as possible' expressed Grandmother's outlook. Growing tall amid the cocksfoot, tiny delicate Cecil Brunner and large lushly-scented deep pink cabbage-roses adorned the close-battened fence, so carefully built by father in the bush-felling days to enclose the two dwellings and small pieces of native bush. This enclosure was a very satisfying world for us children, until we became more adventurous.

As we grew older Sunday School was instituted at Grandma's cottage. We lisped the Catechism and the Twenty-third Psalm obediently but uncomprehendingly though 'lifting up our eyes to the hills' certainly held trenchant meaning. We revelled in Bible stories and stories about bush fires with equal enthusiasm. We heard of how Uncle Rob who was young and frightened had to be coaxed from the windows and the fearful scene of destruction out of doors, with promises of ginger biscuits, 'while the awful red glaring flames and the crashing black logs made a terrible noise. And the fire was just over there, with sparks showering our little home and the smoke making us cough and cry. And Grandmother gave him the *whole tin*,' Annt Nan would tell us. These occasions evidently called forth extreme measures, for ginger biscuits were a dizzy luxury. But this was typical of Grandmother's generosity – once decided upon, it knew no half measures.

Grandmother was a true 'Scotsbyterian', and was determined to impart her version of religious belief together with the social graces to us children, as she had to her own family, growing up as we were in 'pagan freedom in the wilderness' as she saw our situation. When our family had left Southland for the North Island their relatives had gloomily prophesied that they 'would come to no good in that Sodom and Gomorrah of the North' which was their view of the east coast. But we children knew little of all this. Luckily.

Grandmother's character had been formed and tested by a hard life, and her devout faith was sometimes her only standby. She had borne her children far from medical help, and worked hard as a struggling farmer's wife. Sometimes in the Gorge, when Grandfather was absent in Gisborne for a night and the boys were camping out on their bushfalling work, she was alone. Perhaps there would be a startling knock on the kitchen door at dusk. Fearfully, she would open it a little, find a dishevelled figure, bearded and in rags, asking for a 'shakedown'. Mentally saying a swift prayer, she would direct him to the outbuildings and hand him a billy of hot soup from the stock-pot, forever on the range. In the morning there would be a pile of neatly cut wood for the stove, stacked at the doorstep, and the stranger would have vanished, going on his lonely way. Most knew the unwritten codes for such transactions, but there was always the chance that alcohol and too little food would produce a state of irresponsible desperation ... But to Grandmother, the stranger whosoever and whatever he was, was also 'one of God's children'.

Grandma's father had been a captain in the Black Watch regiment before emigrating to New Zealand. He had married a McGregor and settled at Riverton in Southland, where Grandmother was reared. Her uncle and brothers moved to Gisborne where they established fine farms. In the South Island she had met young Arthur Trafford, from Lincolnshire, a sprig from a noble family in Britain, and the couple followed her brothers to Gisborne.

The hard pioneering of her married life was in great contrast to her girlhood. In Southland and in Gisborne, young ladies were taught to sew and paint. Musical evenings were frequently held. Her uncle had a fine voice and knew it. Grandmother, when young, had an impish sense of humour. There was a certain maiden lady of their circle who sang in a dreadful falsetto. Grandmother, hiding her face behind her fan, mischievously suggested that the lady and her brother sing a duet. Uncle was obliged to be polite. The lady, of course, eagerly accepted. Grandmother's face was very pink behind her fan, but she remained outwardly serene, while Uncle inwardly boiled. Such a typical scene from her earlier setting was indeed far removed from the outback life she later led. But she had her memories — and her character. And somehow a piano had been packed into the remote cottage, slung on poles between two draught horses.

We loved everything about Grandmother's house. There were the quickly made girdle scones stirred for our benefit, or oatcake with lard, salty, delicious and crumbly. We had chops for lunch from the open fire where they grilled on a fan-shaped channelled

gridiron which had a little cup in the fork to catch the fat. We loved
the dim recesses of the wardrobes, large and camphor-scented.
They consisted of floor-length blue and mauve chintz curtains
mounted on tawa poles slung across one whole wall of a bedroom.
They made wonderful 'hidey' places. Memorable too, was the soft
luxury of the large bedstead with its deep feather mattress and its
shining brass heads, where we went for a story and a nap as the
afternoon sun drifted behind the hills; and the deerskin and rag
rugs in front of the open fireplace (wide enough to take whole
uncut posts), where we snuggled before a roaring fire while mountain storms pelted the window panes from outside and curtains of
rain swept over the valley. The Maoris had well named the area
'land of the misty gorges', for our rainfall was sometimes over 250
centimetres (100 inches) a year, and for days on end the Gorge
would be washed with rain or overhung with mist, and wreathed
with rainbows. At such times we had recourse to Grandmother's
house, Uncle Stewart's whare, the hayshed, the blacksmith's shed,
or the woolshed, each of which held various sorts of enjoyment.

Mother was especially glad of Grandmother's help with the
older children. In this situation so far from medical help, the
current baby had to be very thoroughly cared for, and the endless
chores of providing nourishing food in a pioneering life accom-
plished efficiently. Often Grandmother bathed us in her cottage in
the large oval galvanized tub in front of the black polished stove
with its gleaming brass tap at the side.

Grandmother was a great believer in the therapeutic value of
warm water for many kinds of upsets, as well as for the inevitable
thistles and stone bruises collected in our roamings. But she was
distressed unto tears when, on one unlucky day, a toddler who
moved too quickly and unexpectedly received a measure of very
hot water on her tender anatomy as Grandmother poured it from
the large white enamel wash jug after turning from the hot tap to
replenish the bath . . . I can still feel the smart and shock of that
burn, and the agony of having it dressed twice weekly with pink
methylated spirits by the district nurse who rode miles to attend
her patient. No risks could be taken with infection and the elders
suffered with me, rebellious though I was. I often hid under the
house when the nurse was expected, I'm sorry to say.

In my time, I hope that my own children have sensed a little of the precious feeling of belonging to a group, for I believe that these patterns are passed on naturally. There is no substitute for that daily contact with varied but warm personalities which was especially ours. The atmosphere of respect for learning, common to the Scots, and the firm moral tone of a rather Calvinistic approach to life were characteristic of my Grandmother. She had been very strict in the upbringing of her own family and Sunday School lessons had been regular and carefully planned. On one occasion her seven year old displeased her by giggling and not paying attention. 'Charles, you are a disgrace to the family,' she told him. 'You shall go to your room, and you shall not be allowed any pudding.' This was a severe punishment, as Charles loved his favourite Queen pudding. His older sister felt sorry for him, and took *her* pudding in. He ate it up greedily and looked at her coldly. 'That was the least you could do after *telling* on me!' he burst out.

So Grandmother's standards had been hard for her children, as they were for us, to live up to. But the forbidding qualities of her character were tempered by a deep natural kindliness and abiding affection for the young.

3

Early Life at Home

There were four of us children. I was the eldest. My brother Larry, next in age to me, was a quiet and resourceful character, always uncomplaining of the many minor hardships we suffered in exploring our environment, such as scratches, knocks, stone bruises, splinters, and frozen hands and feet. Sometimes, as he realized his developing manhood, he was very ready to tease his sisters who were, after all, 'mere girls'. Gael, the third child, was sturdy and good-natured, for the most part trusting that her elder siblings knew best, but also gradually acquiring her independence as a force to be reckoned with in the making of decisions. And Felicity, the youngest, while smaller in stature and not so strong in physique, was stout-hearted and determined to keep up with the rest under any circumstances.

As the eldest, I often had to bear responsibility to the grown-ups for the results of our escapades and was sometimes taken to task if we arrived home late or unduly scratched, dishevelled and dirty. But as little real harm seemed to befall us, more freedom was gradually acquired and we ventured further afield. The rules amongst us were meticulous loyalty and the sharing of anything good that came anybody's way. We nearly always acted as a group, each spontaneously taking a role within it, though, at times, we split into factions according to age, but these rifts were only temporary.

In our early years, our activities mainly centred round the homestead enclosure. We would plan, perhaps, an orchard expedition on a windy autumn day.

'Let's get all the orange pippins in for Mum — they'll only blow down soon,' from Larry.

'Yes, let's! But the PIGS!' cried Gael.

'We'll fix them,' replied Larry confidently. 'We'll block up that.

hole in the pen with branches. Anyway, we can give them a good hiding.'

And so we would set off eagerly with sticks, baskets and boxes. In a corner of the orchard a corrugated iron shelter under the macrocarpas held a pig family of unusual intelligence. At the first shake, as the apples fell and bruised, the pigs smelt them, and nothing could hold them. Down they would rush to the tree, their curly tails flying, and the battle for the apples would commence. Larry, up the tree, having taken the arduous job of shaking the massive old branches, from this vantage point would yell directions to us girls.

'Look out, Judy! Big Red is behind you; he's simply *gobbling* them up!'

I would grab a bigger stick. 'You brute — you brute — take *that* and *that*!'

In sheer fury, we girls would round on the pigs as our indignation at their impudence boiled over. But they would not budge an inch and seemed unconcerned at the heavy whacks being dealt them. They munched greedily, their malevolent little eyes sparkling defiance at us. We would try to coax them away from the tree with some choice apples. 'Pi-i-g, pig pig,' but they were too clever for that. The only tactic left was to snatch the apples from the devouring jaws. We would retire almost exhausted, our baskets half full, the rest of the apples eaten and squashed on the battlefield. We would vow that *next* time we would lock them up somehow. But if we did, they always rooted their way out. Those pigs were our enemies.

We loved our pets, including a family of guinea pigs. We cared for the furry helpless creatures assiduously, bringing their box indoors at night away from the hard frosts. One Easter, Aunt Nan arrived at the farm with her latest acquisition, a small white fox terrier smartly spotted in black, named 'Captain Jinks'. Alas! Within ten minutes he had found the guinea pigs' cage in the orchard, overturned it, and destroyed them all. We sorrowed for days over the row of pathetic little corpses left by Jinks, side by side under the pear tree. Imagine my poor little Patches running, running for his life, only to be pounced on by the terrible Jinks. It just didn't bear thinking of. And that our beloved Aunt Nan should harbour such a monster! The Easter eggs she had kind-heartedly brought did little to console us. It was our first close experience of the immutable ways of Nature and it left us stunned and saddened.

Our family of dolls always interested Gael and me. We would plan a tea-party, setting out the dolls and their floral china tea-set, given us by Grandma, with meticulous care. Slices of bread covered with 'hundreds-and-thousands' made wonderful fare. Then we would persuade Larry to 'Come to afternoon tea'. Being good-natured, he at last consented, but with a gleam in his eye. Soon all the food was gone, the dolls stared as vacantly as ever, and one tiny tea-cup was missing. Gael and I searched frantically, and then began to fret and fuss.

'Larry, *you* had that one, you *must* have seen it!' Long pause.

'Well, Judy — it was so *little* — I swallowed it.'

'You didn't. Don't be awful.'

'Really, I did. It just slipped down.'

Consternation on our part. Perhaps he had really . . . Now what would happen . . . But after a while the wretch produced the cup from his pocket, laughing. Larry didn't much want to be included in 'sissy' dolls' tea-parties . . .

Autumn brought plenty of fruit in the mature old orchard planted by Grandfather, especially apples and pears. The pears were tall, massive, twisty trees. For years they did not bear and Father threatened to axe them. But Mother pleaded for them as she loved their wealth of blossom in the spring and, as she said, it provided food for the bees. Then, one memorable autumn, the pear trees were suddenly laden and thereafter they bore staunchly. Larry was the best at climbing and he collected the biggest and firmest pears to hide in a 'possie' in the grass to ripen. But he always shared his hoard eventually and the fruit was quite delicious, ripened in the warm orchard grass. We loved, too, the fiery bright little apples from a tall seedling tree. Though the grown-ups said they had no flavour, we found them bitter-sweet and good. In spring, a knotty old quince was always smothered in spicy pink and white fragrance and haunted by clouds of bees. We passed it on our way to feed the calves and, somehow, its scent blended with the smell of new milk are forever wedded in my memory.

Correspondence school lessons were sent to us from Wellington. I enjoyed learning to read, fascinated by the large clear letters which held so much meaning. Mother was constantly encouraging, a natural teacher. The school tutor praised my crayon pictures of the apple harvesting which she said, 'conveyed the action most vividly'. I looked forward to each new set of lessons in their strong brown-paper bags with important-looking printed labels, and the tremendous challenge of the world of learning.

We were fortunate in a distant relative in Scotland who took an interest in us 'poor little colonials'. We looked upon her as a real fairy godmother and often wondered what she looked like. She generously sent us large parcels each Christmas, including the best copies she could buy of the children's classics. How we loved these books, poring over the beautiful illustrations on wet days and clamouring for mother's reading of them at night by the lamplight. The adventures of Lewis Carroll's Alice, the 'Swiss Family Robinson', and the Grimm's stories, fired our imaginations, while Kingsley's 'Water Babies' was another definite experience in shaping our philosophy of life. We loved the light-hearted A. A. Milne stories, too, with their pictures of London life. Gael and Felicity were later to travel and have the joy of meeting our 'fairy godmother', a little old Scottish lady rather like Grandma, living in Elgin.

Sundays were 'Grandmother's days' and she believed in there being no 'busyness'. We were to 'pass our time in rest and quietness'. After dinner of roast beef and Yorkshire pudding, and our favourite Queen pudding, she would gather us around the piano for our Bible story. Then we would sing 'Jesus Bids Us Shine' or 'Shall We Gather at the River', or, best of all, 'Onward, Christian Soldiers' with evangelistic fervour. Somehow, after reading Kingsley, we understood the moral approaches of life implicit in 'Mrs Be-done-by-as-you-did' who reminded us a little of Grandma, and 'Mrs Do-as-you-would-be-done-by' whom we immediately identified with Mother. After the hymns we would follow Grandmother reluctantly as she took her sewing bag, her books, and a rug down to a grassy spot under the poplars near the creek. She bade us sit still while she read suitable extracts from the poetry of Robert Burns, from Bunyan's 'Pilgrim's Progress', or quotations from Shakespeare. She held our attention for a while until the clear

glittering water rushing over the amber and grey pebbles between
the boulders beckoned us undeniably. Suddenly we were off, led by
Larry, looking for eels, carefully and quickly up-ending rock after
rock. Grandma would accept the situation, merely saying, 'What
restless children you are today!' and would lie back a little and fall
asleep. Sometimes we returned to the chosen spot to lie prone in
the long grass, looking up into the blue at the millions of thistle-
down, fancying they were fairies all going in the same direction to
a party. Grandma, of course, did not hold with 'fairy nonsense' and
kept our education on the classical side.

In autumn the dusk-filled garden was tempting and we played
until the last light. There were tunnels under the rhododendron
clumps, wonderful for 'hide-and-seek'. Then the sudden dark
of the mountains descended and, fierce anxiety invading us, we
rushed pell-mell indoors to the safe lamplight, pursued by a name-
less Something that might inhabit the rhododendrons . . . Enfolded
by the familiar warmth and faint smell of kerosene, we settled to
games round the fire, sometimes joined by one of the adults. Cards
were our favourite, though they were frowned upon by Grandmother.

One night we all had a severe fright. The casement windows of
the sitting-room were wide open to the warm dusk-filled garden
and we children had settled down inside. Suddenly, all was chaos,
as a wild screeching and flapping heralded the arrival of a pair of
small tawny-feathered owls which flew inside through the open
windows straight towards the Aladdin lamp, missing it by inches,
as it stood on the table, and beat themselves agitatedly about the
room. Mother hated owls as they were the only objects she was
rather superstitious about. She hastily shooed them out, white-
faced the while. Probably we had disturbed them in our play. We
were glad when we were safely tucked in bed that night.

Winter closed in with severe frosts. We would awake to a glis-
tening silvery world outside, condensed moisture sticky and damp
on the blankets, our breath turning to vapour as we huffed and
puffed at each other, windows covered in delicate crystalline frost
tracery. Once out of bed, we passionately longed for the sun to shed
its beneficence upon the sharp blue air so that we could get outside
and walk along the sandy banks where soil-encrusted icicles hung

in great clusters to be crunched satisfyingly under one's boots. Once I had a wonderful idea — perhaps we could make our own ice cream like that we had tasted rapturously on our last flats holiday. We raided the dairy for cream and crept out in the freezing moonlight to place our full-saucered offering on the tankstand. Great anticipation was ours next morning. But what a disappointment! The cold icicled mush was nothing like those elegant cones of memory. Larry had put out a bottle of lemon drink and it had shivered to splinters. Never mind, we thought, the sun was nearly here and soon we would be off again, into the huge outdoors.

During the autumn hunting, a little black wild pig had been brought home in Uncle Ralph's shirt where the jolting of the horse caused it to vomit. He was certainly fond of us to endure such discomfort! The piggy was to replace our guinea pigs and we fondled and fought over him. He seemed to prefer Larry and one frosty night Larry was woken by a rhythmic banging noise. It was Piggy, escaped from his pen, patiently attempting to jump on to Larry's bed on the porch and so, of course, Piggy was smuggled under the blankets until the grown-ups became aware of the muffled squeaks and grunts emanating occasionally from the bed. They decreed this altogether too primitive. A *pig* in *bed*! Disgraceful! And Piggy was again confined to his box at night.

Of all the adults, Mother was the most understanding of our love of natural elements. We often arrived at the back porch dripping and muddy after playing all morning on a sandy bank making large mud pies decorated with ferns and daisies. Or, perhaps, we would take the garden trowels to excavate blue clay from a fascinating hollow, where the oozy cold clay formed the whole bank. It was wonderful for making model animals, small canoes and bowls to be dried later on by the hob of the open fire. 'House-building' was, at intervals, a fever. We would collect fallen ponga logs, patiently heaping them between convenient saplings to build walls. Of course, the roof always collapsed. But we made wonderful couches and beds from the dry bracken, each claiming a corner of the hut for his own. Mother quietly saved a number of sacks and took them, with hammer and nails, to the lacebark grove one memorable day. Using the trees as corner poles, she soon had us a house complete with rooms formed by the sacking walls. Our dolls and household odds and ends were transferred there, which activity kept us happy for days. Mother was a natural with children and, considering the mores of the age, was far advanced in her outlook on child rearing. In our younger days she encouraged creativity in us in every way she could, always tolerant of the messes we made with dough, flour paste and scissors on wet days, and later encouraging us to write for school magazines, make, or sew things. She herself was a creative and vital person, interested in people and invariably able to understand and befriend them. She told her friends she believed in a policy of 'watchful neglect' with us, which somewhat scandalized some who forecast that we would be completely spoilt or end in disaster. Grandmother was often uneasy, too. But she was getting old and was rather tired nowadays and, though always interested and alert in our presence, she preferred to leave our disciplining, or lack of it, to others. Between them, they shaped our outlook and image of life. One of Mother's more homely mottoes was 'Do the task that's next you, though it's dull at whiles. Helping when you meet them, lame dogs over stiles'. (And she never 'pushed' them!) And there, in this simple acceptance of the situation in which one found oneself in life, lay much of the strength of endurance found in such pioneer women as Mother and Grandmother.

Father, true to his Scottish upbringing, was painstakingly conscientious about details, intolerant of disorder of any kind. But he had the hospitality of the clansman and, in personal relationships, he always looked for the man beneath the rank. Both Mother and Father admired Kipling and his verse; 'Playing the Game' was hung in a prominent place in the living room and probably had its quiet effect upon each one of us. We were never molly-coddled.

The roaring, windy days of winter brought the joy of climbing the conifers on the orchard ridge from the tops of which we could overlook the house and garden. As the slender branches lifted and swayed, we thrilled to the sense of power in the wind. Tiring at last, we would run home, hot, scratched, and bruised with our hands and clothes reeking of pungent pine resin.

A rubble slip, left by the road makers, was just along the road from the homestead. We loved to slide and jump in the soft fine rubble which trickled constantly from a fearsome bald precipice reaching twenty metres above our heads. We would rush up the slip, reaching the top by sheer momentum, only to be catapulted downwards as the soft medium slid away from under us, filling the water-table carefully tended by Old Sandy, the roadman. Next time we met, he would give us a tongue-thrashing, adding that we would probably be killed by a rolling stone. And Grandmother would shake her head over us, sadly.

Much of life for the adults was centred on providing the necessities of living and we saw little of them except at meals and in the evenings when games with us brought some relaxation for them, too. Father had a fine stamp collection which interested us greatly.

Bread was made from home-made yeast twice weekly and butter was made as well. Large pans of milk were set in the dairy after the milk was heated to scalding point. The cream then formed a thick layer on top to be skimmed off with a flat perforated saucer-shaped metal utensil, and collected in a cream can. Much churning in the heavy wooden churn completed the operation of butter-making, and Grandma always took a hand at turning it. Bacon was cured and the sides had to be rubbed with saltpetre and brown sugar daily, an arduous task on frosty mornings. All jams, pickles and perhaps a hundred or so jars of preserved fruit had to be 'put up' each autumn. Soap was made in the large washing copper in the lean-to at the side of the house. We thought it was beautiful as we gazed into its liquid amber depths, and were fascinated at its firm whiteness next morning, its clean odour of citronella and Mother's deft way of carving it into neat blocks with the biggest knife she possessed. Mother had beautiful hands but this life sadly roughened them.

Mother's one luxury was her garden which she loved and planted lavishly with the old-fashioned shrubs she had known in her youth. Only the hardiest survived the mountain climate but in spring and early summer, loveliness abounded. Mauve rhododendrons, pink and white weigelas, buddleias, the dainty white bridal deutzia, and masses of fragrant Dorothy Perkins roses all flourished. Grandfather had planted a background of oaks and chestnuts and now primroses nestled at their feet. Much later, when away at school and homesick, I was to love Browning's verse 'Oh to be in England Now that April's there', from 'Home-

Thoughts from Abroad' for the picture of home that it conjured up for me. And somehow his 'gaudy melon flower' seemed appropriate to the plain land with its semitropical, sometimes sultry climate. I longed quite desperately at times for the freshness of the mountains.

In the homestead garden, rock borders were made from flat waterworn stones from the creeks, sometimes laboriously carried home by us children, a task we enjoyed. In autumn, red-orange dahlias, purple Michaelmas daisies, and golden rod grew in a tangle of brilliant colour in all the corners of the enclosure and the old trees, poplars, oaks, chestnuts and viburnums turned on a riot of tawny reds and golds as the frost claimed them. Again, in later years, I was to love William Carruth's 'Each in His Own Tongue' which expresses so beautifully the wonder and awe of the passing seasons:

> 'A haze on the far horizon,
> The infinite tender sky,
> The ripe, rich tint of the corn fields,
> And the wild geese flying high;
> All over upland and lowland
> The charm of the golden rod:
> Some of us call it Autumn
> And others call it God . . .'

Mother aspired to a fernery where, over the years, bush treasures were transplanted. In spring the little dell was wreathed and carpeted with English hyacinths in which bumble-bees revelled in drunken fervour. Here, too, English lycopodium, a feathery ground creeper, grew. This dell was Mother's pride.

Father planted a variety of conifers and choice mountain shrubs, and he took great pride in the vegetable garden, manuring it with woolshed daggings and refuse from the slaughterhouse. We were allowed to eat raw carrots freely, and ripe yellow gooseberries, luscious raspberries, and loganberries were plentiful in season. Rhubarb grew in giant stalks; when stewed and eaten with Mother's pastry squares and clotted cream it was a memorable lunch during the hot shearing days of early summer. Each shearing time Father brewed raisin and hop beer in cool earthenware crocks, later bottling it. It was reasonably mild, though Grandmother forbade us even to *sip* it. But occasionally, a bottle cork rapped the ceiling, perhaps in the dead of night. 'A good brew', Father would say, next morning, while poor Mother mopped up the frothy creamy mess. The shearers certainly appreciated it, and in those years nobody was ever drunk.

Besides the usual farm work, stove and fire wood had to be collected and split, which absorbed perhaps two days a week of Father's time, and much groyne-making was undertaken. These long narrow stone groynes snaking along the creek edges, involved tremendous manual labour. A heavy gauge wire mesh was first laid in a trench, then the stones were piled in, barrow-load by barrow-load, until the groyne was more than half a metre above ground. The sides of the mesh were then folded across on top of the stones and joined in the centre with wire lacing. The whole formed a wonderful protection against the wayward creeks which became raging mountain torrents in flood-time, likely to rush out of their courses and erode any man-made obstacle. The woolshed, cow-shed, and slaughterhouse, and their main access routes, had to be thus protected. The homestead and buildings stood near the confluence of three creeks and almost the whole of the little valley could be awash in a flood. We children liked running along the groynes collecting the flotsam and jetsam and watching the boiling torrent as it subsided, but not for long as the wire and stones were hard and bruised our feet, tough-soled though they were.

Meanwhile, the endless farm work went on: post splitting, fencing, building repairs, ploughing the steepish slopes with the two-horse plough for potatoes or swedes. A middle-aged bachelor relative of Scottish extraction had come from the south and taken up employment with the family; Cousin Stewart was a loyal and willing helper. Although rather taciturn, we soon found that he had a soft regard for us children and we would sometimes share his evening fire in the whare to hear stories of his boyhood in 'the South'. He was another notable in our gallery of personalities. We were poor I suppose, but we children didn't worry much — though I remember seeing a beautifully neat two-storeyed suburban house in Gisborne and thinking in my foolish childish way, I would love to live in that. I would, of course, have loathed it after a very short time.

The days of our early childhood drifted by. Two new rooms were added to the cottage and we became great friends with the young carpenter engaged for the building. One room was for us two older girls, with pretty floral paper, a curtained wardrobe in a corner, and shelves for our beloved books especially bought for us by Grandmother. The other room was for a recently arrived 'lady help'. She was a pleasant young woman, much given to uncontrollable fits of laughter in moments of tension. Part of her duties was to help Larry and me with our Correspondence School lessons. But somehow, we found that her spelling differed from ours and we argued a lot. Mother soon found out that she had left school after attaining Standard Three. Also she spent much time chatting animatedly with the young carpenter, and she was soon relegated to the dairy and kitchen tasks.

4

The Roadmaking

Matawai and Motu, both lusty young sawmilling settlements, were our nearest centres, Matawai being sixteen kilometres distant from the homestead, and what rough miles they were.

Matawai had sprung up in the usual sprawling fashion of settlements in New Zealand. It was situated at the junction of the Motu and Gorge roads. Its small cluster of shops straggled down the main street, its surface pumice-dusty in summer and deeply muddy in winter after the snowfalls. Great pride was taken by the residents of the infant settlement in its official buildings, the post office and the school, and each boasted a flag-pole.

One store was kept by a rather learned Englishman, a dry character, who was an avid stamp collector. I don't think he was very adept at the business of making profits, but he was kind and 'obliging', as the locals said, to everyone and very well liked. Probably the feeling of simply supplying needed commodities and his habit of quietly offering what he felt was good advice to all in trouble, was compensation enough for him as he had no kith or kin. Within the dim recesses of his precincts there was a staggering and apparently chaotic array of wares both for households — from kerosene stoves to mousetraps — and for bushfelling and roadmaking, including cross-cut saws of many lengths, axes, slashers, picks and shovels, and horse gear. The blended musty fragrance of strong tobacco, kerosene, stored cereals and pickles, vinegar and mothballs, combined to produce the nostalgic and unmistakable aroma of a country store.

Across the road was the blacksmith, a strong, cheerful man, and next to him the saddler and shoe-mender, a little old hunched-up man forever diligent in his hand-stitching and saddle-repairing which was of superb craftsmanship. His perennial cough was always worse in the severe winters. Nearer the railway station and stockyards stood the village hall, scene of rowdy card evenings when the gangs from the bush-milling centres came into 'town' on Saturday nights on their sturdy bush-bred nags. Above the village there still broods the vast mist-wreathed bulk of 'Mt Misery', so named by the settlers, perhaps as an ironic comment upon the toughness of their struggle for a living.

A rough road extended beyond Matawai to the Motu river crossing at the foot of the Hill (which came to be known as 'Trafford's Hill'), while the railway from Gisborne had been constructed to Otoko, then Matawai, and later to Motu. Roading and communication northwards were extending but the Hill and the range of which it formed a part was one of the major challenges to the engineers and surveyors seeking a northern outlet for Gisborne and the east coast province. A rough bridle track wound up and over it, down past our homestead and further into the Gorge. Eventually, in the late twenties, the road followed this track, but not before the merits of the existing alternative route over the Motu hills were carefully weighed. And, of course, there was local lobbying. My father and others personally conducted surveyors over the Gorge route and were persuasive about its practicability. It was likely to cost less, there was only one major hill, and it was direct and shortest — all of which were salient points. The Motu settlers claimed equally emphatically that their hills were safer as there would be fewer slips and washouts. Estimated costs were eventually the deciding factor, and the Motu settlers succumbed with reasonable grace as their route was to be maintained as an alternative. But, in later years, after the hotel was moved to Matawai to cater for the service-car trade through the Waioeka (for, of course, the Gisborne-based company chose the shorter route), there was inevitably some resentment, and the leaders in each district thereafter scrupulously guarded their rights on local committees. And Father was unpopular in certain households on the isolated Motu farms.

The Hill, as I have said, was an understatement; it was a great divide, with its summit towering to 700 metres altitude, shaggy with bush and bristling with rocky outcrops, and its slab sides precariously spanned by a narrow bridle track. In places like the 'Rocky Cutting' half-way down on the Gorge side, the narrow shelf dropped sheer away over thirty metres to the creek bed below. Equipment for the roading job would consist of little more than picks, shovels and gelignite, combined with human effort and willingness to work on the part of the men, for now, in the early nineteen thirties, the shadow of serious unemployment lay over New Zealand. After a visit from a Minister of the Crown who, with his party, was entertained in the farm sitting-room at Raysburn, the decision was taken to proceed with the Gorge route and Father and the other settlers pledged every support to the roadmakers.

Slowly the gangs crept upwards from the end of the existing road which reached to the Motu River and a 'modern 14 ft road', according to the standards of the day, was carved out over the Hill. My family, eager to see the advance of this life-line, lent every possible assistance such as pack-horses, a dray, a buggy and, when it was bought, our new Model T Ford, the first in the district. My mother was the only driver in the family and our car was used to help shift the workers camps, as the road progressed. So the little car, hood folded down, was often piled high with camp gear, boards and tents. Mother, a slender but dauntless figure, could clamber over the assortment of bric-a-brac and squeeze into the tiny space left behind the wheel. She was truly proud of her efficiency and for a time was on the Public Works Department's payroll as a driver, a distinction in those post-Victorian days. The men were all her 'fans' for they admired her wit, good sense, and pluck. Sometimes she had to drive across planks spanning a complete washout in the shelf of a road, or pick a way for the vehicle round the massive boulders of a slip (luckily, these early cars had a high chassis after the horse-drawn vehicle style). Several gangers would stand with crowbars at the ready on the creek side of the slip, in order to heave the little car back manually, should it slide sideways, in danger of crashing down into the creek bed, perhaps twelve metres below. Mother was warned that she must be prepared to jump! On these occasions we children had to get out and watch from a safe distance, our hearts bumping painfully, our eyes glued to the little car in an agony of apprehension. Would it, would it slip sideways . . . But Mother always got over and the gangers would help us, in a fatherly and most respectful manner, to cross on foot.

The hard toil of the men continued day by day, blasting, picking

and shovelling each yard out of the sheer rock faces. Most were
fugitives from the towns since the closing in of the Depression.
Occasionally a well-educated 'remittance man' or assisted immi-
grant from England arrived, usually staying but a short while. He
would treat Mother with conspicuous gallantry, lifting his battered
hat every few minutes but, of course, was also usually a complete
misfit with the other men. Scots, Swedes, Irish, an occasional
Maori — they were all of the hardy variety of human, or were soon
packing their swags to leave. At one time, there were eighty men in
the Gorge employed on the roadmaking, camped in fairly primitive
canvastown conditions.

Many a feud had to be tactfully investigated by the young engineer in charge. He was quartered at the homestead and was
greatly liked by us all as he always had great good humour, but his
resources were often tested. Isolation, crowded quarters, the mixture of personalities, often with the addition of homemade 'moon-
shine', bred stormy scenes.

Pay-day brought a sort of release. The men gathered at our
homestead to collect their earnings from the engineer/paymaster.
Our old gramophone would be much in demand and we children
responded with alacrity to requests to put on records produced by
the men, such as one called, from memory, 'Big Rock Candy Mountains'. Apparently it had the right brand of humour with its refrain:
> 'In the Big Rock Candy Mountains
> They never change their socks,
> And little streams of alcohol
> Come trickling down the rocks'

As did the even more ribald:
> 'Hallelujah, I'm a bum,
> Hallelujah, bum again.
> Hallelujah, giv' us a handout
> To revive us again.'

by a certain Joe Hill, a parody of a Salvation Army hymn.

Inevitably, nostalgia set in as the men thought of homes and
families and 'The Weeping Willow Tree' brought moist eyes. The
party continued at camp around the wooden keg which had been
procured with great feats of daring by swimming it across the Motu.
One bad night, when passions were truly raised, a certain Big Jim

who was still sober enough to realize that the evening was going to end in tragedy, dramatically broached it with an axe, leaving the whisky gushing forth accompanied by shouts, tears and curses from the rest. He then fled to the homestead. The young engineer, a truly resourceful man, escorted him back next morning when tempers had cooled, and he was reinstated as a 'mate' again, amid grumbling and sour looks.

When it was discovered by the elders that we had been entertaining the gangers, Grandma was forthright. 'Disgraceful music!' she pronounced and, after much lecturing, we were banished to our lessons. The records disappeared and were found put to good use stopping draughts in her corrugated iron fowl house as, of course, she would never have actually destroyed another person's property. Grandmother administered spiritual and bodily sustenance to the men in the form of some Presbyterian pamphlets and a huge enamel teapot of tea. But *we* had tasted *Life*.

By this time the road was being formed but a stone's throw from the homestead, across the creek. Whenever there was a warning shout from the men, we children were hastily gathered indoors and the subsequent thunder of exploding gelignite produced showers of rubble over house, lawn and garden. It always interrupted a game and, thinking the grown-ups fussy, we deliberately dawdled to watch the fun. But after one such episode, Charlie, a big quiet man, appeared, white-faced and trembling all over. He was almost incoherent but, by degrees, it was learnt that he and his mate had taken shelter behind a rock ridge and a falling piece of rock had lobbed over the ridge and landed directly where his mate was standing. Shortly, there followed a pathetic little procession as the young man was carried to the homestead on a stretcher. He lay immobile with his hat over his face, his bushy red beard protruding from under its brim. Father quickly examined him and had to tell Charlie that he was 'beyond all mortal help'. At this, the tears streamed down Charlie's face. We children felt sick and rushed away to our hiding place in the clump of bamboo, our refuge in time of trouble. No more work was done by the men that week. They were completely unnerved as no one had ever thought such a thing would really happen.

Mother was called to the camps many times to perform nursing

duties, dealing with bad cuts and bruises until the help of the
district nurse could be obtained. One night a desperate Maori
husband claimed her assistance at a childbirth, and I remember her
returning at dawn, grey-looking with anxiety and lack of sleep. No
comments were made to us but we guessed the facts from the
conversation and as soon as we could we hurried over to the camp
at Smith's Creek. All was well, and we were allowed to nurse the
darling baby, and we later watched the bathing process. The mother gave us tins of sweetened condensed milk which we consumed
on the spot. Ehu, a five-year-old, disappeared outside and after
digging a while in a nearby rotten log brought in one of his choice
delicacies for us, some wriggling huhu grubs. Nudged by the others,
and remembering Grandmother's training, I had to accept them
with solemn appreciation. I think I did actually eat one after insis-
ting that it be first despatched, and Ehu commented 'Good, eh?'
Grandmother visited the mother too, to read appropriate passages
from the Bible, in thankfulness for her safe delivery.

The Gorge was then wild and untamed, and lovely by any standard. The steep slopes on either side of the creek were lined with
groves of tree ferns massed in delicate cascades. Lofty kahikatea,
rimu and tawa adorned the ridges and the small watercourses were
hidden and overhung by graceful konini, karamu, makomako,
five-finger and all the diverse species of shrubs, vines, and small
trees found in the North Island's rain forests. In the lower Gorge
near the coast, handsome nikau palms tossed their varnished
fronds proudly and the river below in its granite-lined bed foamed
and tumbled in crystalline white and green waters about craggy
rock formations, at intervals emerging into deep cool green-shaded
pools where rainbow trout lay undisturbed on hot summer days.

Water jets from tiny tinkling creeks, lined with a myriad of
mosses, studded the banks with beauty and at night these were
thickly haunted with glow-worms. On a summer day, sunlight and
shade lay in patches across the narrow bridle track, and bellbird
and tui sent their joyful echoes across the river. All day the cicadas'
chorus provided a background of friendly sound until the still
evening hour when the crickets continued it with only an occasional sudden jarring note from a morepork. Bush scents of rangi-
ora, kumerahou, beech, tawa and tarata mingled with the pungence

of pennyroyal growing along the water's edge and in the grassy spaces along the track. The sudden gleam of a trout in a still pool, or as a silver flick in white water rapids, challenged our quick young eyes. Over all, there was a sense of peace and solitude, a sense of the primeval silence of the waiting centuries, of the perfection of growth and renewal in the untouched New Zealand bush.

Of necessity, the roadmakers hacked through all this. Gisborne had been isolated from the rest of New Zealand for many of its formative years because of the difficulty of road access. The young engineers and the roadmakers were thus challenged to their utmost at all stages of the road building. The cost was enormous, even in later years with the use of modern machinery. But by 1930 the Waioeka road had been cut through to the coast, although the unbridged crossings and the constant slips were to be formidable hazards to the traveller for years to come.

The scars healed in time. Today, except for the swinging curves of bitumen, the scenery is little changed. But the home of our youth is gone, destroyed by fire, and the creek beds have risen, changing the face of the little valley that was our world. But the childhood contact with the healing peace of the bush became forever part of us, a rare privilege. And a new fraternity of the Gorge replaced the roadmakers, composed of stock drovers, service-car drivers, freight-car operators, commercial travellers, visiting professional men, and those who loved to travel the wilder places of New Zealand. Whenever such individuals struck upon the Waioeka in conversation, occupation and status were forgotten, and talk of 'the Manganuku' (a notorious crossing) and the like took over.

In considering the tremendous endeavour by so many individuals to overcome the roadmaking challenge, one's admiration goes to the early surveyors and engineers: to such men as William Hickey, living at the Opotiki end of the Gorge and riding five days a week out to his job as gang paymaster and roading engineer, carrying always a revolver with his money satchel, and to Mr. William Brook a gentle steadfast man who rode countless trips from Motu, at the Gisborne end, surveying and pegging the Waioeka Gorge road over the Hill, as a preliminary to its commencement by public works gangs. His headquarters were at Gisborne, long miles and countless river crossings away. The Brooks and my family were the greatest of friends. Mrs Brook, a gently bred, well educated young woman brought up her family of young children in outback conditions and gave them faith in their Christian heritage, a love of books, music and the cultivated mind, and a quiet determination to be their own persons. Eventually they all became much loved, respected, and talented urban dwellers.

5

School

After the failure of the lady help to tutor our Correspondence
School lessons, our parents talked unceasingly of the problems of
our education. After much discussion of the dangers and disadvan-
tages, and weighing of these against the importance of our acquiring a formal education, Mother and Father decided to enlist the aid
of the service-car drivers in conveying us to Wairata, the nearest
school, sixteen kilometres distant towards Opotiki and in the middle of the Gorge. The service-cars, to us a link with the mysterious
outside world, had been running twice daily for some months now.
The morning car at 9 a.m. fitted well enough, though we would
arrive at school three-quarters of an hour late, but we would have
to wait until 7.30 p.m. for the homeward car. Perhaps it could be
arranged for a kindly roadman's wife, whose cottage was near the
school, to watch over us between school and home and to bed us
for the night should there be a slip on one of the many bluffs and
the car fail to get through.

We two older children listened to all this with apprehensive
ears. But in a way it would be an adventure: fancy actually travelling in a White Star limousine amid all the passengers from the
outside world!

One fateful morning, then, Father walked over the creek to the
road by the direct route formed by a large fallen tree log which
acted as a bridge. He was accompanied by 'Pompey', our tiny Pome-
ranian dog who usually trotted over alone and collected the morning paper, catching it neatly as the service-car driver slowed and
threw it to him, much to the delight of the passengers who were
truly amused by this little tableau.

This time the car stopped, and there was quite a long conversation between Father and the driver. I like to think that it was
'Dick' Whittington, a character with a heart of gold, who thus

casually consented to take us two eldest children on board the car, 'as long as I can squeeze them in', and convey us to school. The cars were not big and had an attached luggage box outside the coach, lined on top with a low handrail. Here, parcels and luggage were carried. Take us the drivers did, even though we often had to be deposited along with the parcels on top of the luggage box, with strict injunctions to 'hang on tight!' to the handrail. We came to enjoy the times when the inside was full, as our interest in the passengers palled after a while and we loved travelling our beloved Gorge in the fresh scented mornings from such a vantage point. As far as I know, money or fares were never mentioned. As for insurance — nobody brought up such complexities! Of course, the settlers and service-car drivers were mutually dependant in so many ways. And my family were especially able to help, situated as they were at the foot of the Hill which was a severe test for most cars of the time. Many a cup of tea was dispensed by Mother and Grandmother to the service-car passengers, temporarily delayed by a slip on the Hill or a flooded creek, and bored, cold, and tired by their long journey.

And so preparations for sending us to school were made. Warm woollen frocks were sewn for me, to be accompanied by a red petticoat lovingly crocheted in thick ply wool by Grandmother, and heavy black stockings. New hair ribbons for my two long dark braids were proudly pressed. Larry had to have long grey stocking hose, and new jerseys, and trousers with a fly, of which he was extremely proud. Each morning we watched the road cutting across part of the Hill, visible from the tiny sitting-room window by the fireplace. When the service-car appeared in view , grey-looking and tiny, we dashed nimbly across the log bridge to the road, always fearful of missing it. Soon it arrived, resplendent in dark blue glossy paint, with a gold checkered band and a crest above the windscreen. Inside were notices in large black print which we traced out moving our lips silently 'No Smoking', 'Please Do Not Expectorate'.

'What is expectorate?' we asked mother when we got home.

'A polite word for spitting,' she replied, laughing at our puzzlement.

Did people *spit* in service-cars? They always seemed quite nice when they came in to morning tea and often gave us things . . . On many a morning we waited in vain until about 10 a.m. when (what joy!) the grown-ups decreed we could be let off school as the car had been delayed. Really wet days, too, brought wonderful holidays as the risk of slips and of the car not returning was too great. We would joyfully doff our now hated school clothes and be off at the first lifting of the rain clouds to explore and paddle in our tiny creeks, now swollen to rushing torrents and fascinating to play in.

On the whole, school was a happy experience. But these first few months were quite ghastly. We were teased unmercifully about our new clothes, my pigtails, our 'funny' way of coming to school (due, perhaps to misplaced jealousy!). In fact, our total strangeness offended everyone else at first as the majority were from road-keepers' homes and they had few contacts with settlers' children outside school. In the way of school children, the world over (or, at least, in Western societies), insults pertaining to anal and erotic functions were flung at us. At first we were dumb and horror-struck as we had always had a casual acceptance of such things. But after a while we managed to shut our ears and be on the look-out for any distraction to divert our tormentors. And we learned to pull the most horrible faces when tightly cornered and to bluff our way out. Luckily, for some reason, we were never physically assaulted, though such things were common in such schools.

Wairata was a sole-charge school with about fifteen pupils. The school was a neat little building with its playground edged with thick bush from which a steep bluff fell away to the riverbed on one side. The schoolground was situated between the river forks and reached by a bridge from the main road and a paddock for ponies adjoined it. There is still a tiny school there and the surroundings have altered little.

The first school had been held in a settler's home nearby and the present building, of creosoted pit-sawn timber, had been erected by the settlers. It was draughty, and had a slab concrete chimney which smoked. Shortly after we started school, and after much official correspondence between settlers and Education Board, a change for the better was made. A fine new school was built by the Auckland Education Board. It was a neat cream-painted building with large sunny windows, surrounded by concrete and with a long seat on an outside wall. A flagpole proudly surmounted the name-plate on which was painted 'Wairata School' in large letters. The New Zealand ensign was flown on King's Birthday, when we all trooped out to salute it, but not without some preliminary scuffling and giggling.

A coloured globe of the world stood in a corner of the classroom and I took great satisfaction in the pink areas which covered so much of it. We were British. This point of view had been rein-forced at home. My readings of the *Boy's Own Paper*, in which the heroes suffered the most awful privations in darkest Africa and South America at the hands of strange tribes but always managed to return home safely to green beloved England, clean sheets and civilization, formed my attitudes for life. Perhaps we were too British for the raw social amalgam of the Gorge.

The compassionate young teacher did his best for us, especially when he found that we were well advanced with our school lessons. But this, of course, added to our offensiveness, so we learned to be 'mum' often, though we knew the answers. Apparently we were supposed to be 'rich' people and when we protested innocence of this charge, being totally amazed by it, they said, 'Well, your father must have *hidden* all his money.' After an agony of time we were partly accepted and happily sang our times tables along with the rest, sitting on the bench outside the school on the sunny summer days, accompanied by a fervent cicada chorus from the nearby bush.

Playing in the bush was wonderful. We swung high and wide on the supple-jack vines which formed a kind of maypole, this being a traditional Maori pastime. We played 'Cavaliers and Round-heads' in the tall bracken, near the edge of the bluff, each party stalking the other with deadly concentration. (What a trans-portation of culture!) Or we played cricket on the tiny pitch where girls, of course, were barely tolerated but had to be included to make up two teams. I well remember big Bruce in Standard Six, (to us a kind of deity) being utterly disgusted because the Primers always dropped the ball after running eagerly and hopefully to catch it.

Waiting for the late car after school dismayed us. Although the road-man's wife was a kindly person, their house was tiny and she had her own problems. And, although she sometimes gave us wonderful vanilla-flavoured buns and cups of cocoa, we mostly waited by the roadside. As the Gorge darkened early, especially in winter, and perhaps a lone morepork hooted, we felt the atmosphere changing and becoming sinister. We longed with all our hearts for home. There was by now, a fairly steady stream of private cars passing through this route and, one evening, in sheer desperation we summoned the courage to halt one, waving our arms or making a 'Stop' sign. Hesitatingly we asked for 'a ride home'. Our earnest near-tearful faces must have convinced the occupants of the genuine nature of the request and it was cheerfully complied with. Nearing home, our spirits rose and we ran lightfootedly over the bridge, the folk in the car looking on, and we were soon tucking into a slab of home-baked bread and gooseberry jam. From that day on we usually arrived home jubilantly with the first 'lift' we could manage.

The grown-ups seemed to view this development with the greatest anxiety. We were warned never to stop a car without a lady in it. But we couldn't always ascertain this seemingly important detail and found that truck drivers had kind hearts. We couldn't see why 'they' were fussing. We'd *got home* and weren't they pleased to see us? At this, mother threw her arms around us and seemed almost in tears. And so we were entrusted to Heaven, and I've no doubt Grandmother prayed daily for our safety. We became quite famous as 'those children that we picked up in that terrible Gorge — really entertaining little kids — they told us all about the Gorge and the countryside.' We children learnt to know the travelling public and in those days it was apparently quite trustworthy as we were never embarrassed or offended in any way. We were often given sweets, fruit, even a dear little pottery brooch for me from a rather gushing, but warm-hearted, lady who said in an aside to her husband, 'Poor, dear little things, what a life!' which rather puzzled us.

At school we liked the generosity and naturalness of the Maori children and recognized them as kindred in that their love of life matched our own. We sometimes asked two Maori sisters home for weekends. We longed to sample the kie kie fruit they raved about, and swim and eel in the lovely deep green-shaded pools in the river behind the cottage where they lived, but somehow we never got to

stay with them. At school as we became one of the group, we loved
the way their dark eyes became expressive and mysterious when
they told us about Maori customs and the tapu as we sat close
together in the playground.

Sewing lessons for the younger girls were held at a nearby farm-
house by a little lady of Scottish extraction who was very approved
by my Grandmother and who was willing to help us through our
struggles to learn blanket and lazy-daisy stitches, sewing on little
pieces of canvas. Her house was pleasant, surrounded by well-
tended gardens and stone-flagged paths and she gave us nice afternoon tea in a most decorous fashion. Unfortunately, to reach her
house, we of Standards One or Two had to cross the river in a cage
suspended on a cable, escorted by two Standard Six boys, and
without Larry I felt particularly vulnerable. I was heart-rendingly
frightened when the two boys would stop the cage in midstream
nine metres above the rocky riverbed and rock it vigorously. After
the screams and tears had been investigated by our hostess (who
was genuinely shocked and who missed nothing), the boys were
soundly caned and we were taken over with more decorum and
safety!

We came to like and deeply admire our teachers who were from
the ranks of the keenest young men in the service, out for sole-
charge experience with, perhaps, an educational background of
Auckland Grammar School and Teachers' College. I had always
loved reading and now I realized that I, too, could write intelligible
stories, though sometimes I think they were a source of puzzlement
for most of the other children, who would much rather be outdoors anyway, except perhaps my Maori friends with their sensi-
bility towards expression in song, dance and poetry. I can still
remember one Maori boy's spirited rendering of Masefield's 'Sea
Fever' which he loved, though at first the language must have been
strange to him. One week, the essay topic was 'The journey of a
river' and, inspired by Tennyson's lovely lines from 'The Brook',
written from the fen country of his native Lincolnshire:

> 'I come from haunts of coot and hern,
> I make a sudden sally
> And sparkle out among the fern,
> To bicker down a valley.'

I wrote with passion my own version of our lovely bush streams according to my poetic experience. The teacher read it aloud and, crowning praise, put it in his pocket to be 'sent away'. And so I suppose began for me a teaching career which was to include sole-charge experience and, later, writing, though I little knew it at the time.

The school had a copy of the ten volumes of Arthur Mee's *The Children's Encyclopedia* which I eagerly digested in wet lunch hours, and father had twelve bound volumes of *'Life'* magazine which I read rather more surreptitiously, along with volumes of the *Boy's Own Paper* and the aunts' *Girl's School Stories* at home, and later the homestead's small collection of classics, such as *Jane Eyre*, Dickens, Scott, Conrad, and Rider Haggard.

Break-up day at the year's end was a wonderful community experience. The school was scrubbed with a will, inside and out. We smaller fry were given the task of polishing the brass ink-wells to a glorious golden reflectiveness. It felt like finding an unexpected treasure, so transformed were they. The older children scraped the desk surfaces to irreproachable kauri whiteness with slivers of glass. The school gardens were tidied meticulously. These consisted of a special area, including a sloping bank, which was enclosed from horses and terraced with ponga-edged beds. Masses of pinks, mignonette and sweet-william, sent up incense to the midday sun pouring its benevolence into the valley. And we worked here, perspiring and enthusiastic, until not a weed remained. A young pine tree, glossy green in the summer sunlight, was erected in the centre of the playground and its branches loaded with presents, mostly unwrapped. Many had been made by the parents, and especially the Scottish lady, for she had no children of her own. Great was the conjecture, as we gazed at the tree beforehand, as to whom would be given what. One year, I particularly coveted a quaint little inflatable rubber tortoise for water-play and, to my unbelieving joy, I received it, while Gael was given the huge floppy rag doll with long yellow wool plaits which she had longed for.

Luncheon consisted of a hangi made with sweet-smelling manuka wood in the shade of the bush edge. The Maori people took charge of this and the beautifully cooked food was generously pressed upon us, together with gallons of raspberry cordial and ice cream especially imported in chilled containers for the occasion. Then we retired to the schoolroom to sing or say individual verses, assiduously learnt for the occasion but now, alas, stumblingly produced. One master had composed a song which was sung lustily and was enthused over by the parents:

>'There's a happy little spot
>By a rocky little stream
>It is Wai-i-rata!
>And for happiness and jollity
>It surely is supreme
>Is Wai-i-rata etc.

Break-up day was pure delight.

The service-car company instituted a midday car service, travelling back from Opotiki. It passed the school at 1.15 p.m. and so our days of waiting by the roadside were over. The driver blasted his horn when rounding the bluff across the river from the school. This was the signal for us to down books and pencils, grab our bags, and rush madly down the bush track and across the bridge to the road – much to the envy of the rest. The drivers were proud of keeping on schedule and would brook no dawdling on our part; we seldom missed the car but were woebegone when we did. Felicity was at school and a roadman's family had joined us so we were now eight on the service-car. And we loved school.

6

Holidays on the Flats

As the September holidays approached, we four children began to look forward eagerly to our annual stay at 'Riverford', Mother's family home near Ormond on the Gisborne plain land. And during the short closed-in days of mid-winter in the Gorge, with its bitter frosts, early dark and long periods of rain and mist, the prospect of spring on the wide sunny flats was delightful indeed. From our earliest days we revelled in these contrasts. Although by September, even in the Gorge, the days were beginning to lengthen, spring was in full flush on the flats and the very air seemed to dance and vibrate with it. Everywhere was the tender green of new grass and the paler green of the bursting willows with their long weeping strands. The warm sun sparkled on the broad lazy river behind the serried rows of new-leafed lombardy poplars, and in the long evenings it set rosily behind a strangely distant horizon.

The well planted old homestead garden was full of scent and colour, and the masses of jonquils and daffodils, the huge bee-haunted camellia trees laden with pink and white rosettes, and the mauve and pink rhododendrons and azaleas all combined to produce sensuous delight for us. In the paddocks, lambs and calves were everywhere and in the homestead sheds there was usually a new litter of puppies.

But first, we had to accomplish the journey, an exciting adventure in itself. Mother tried to choose a fine day. The night before, shoes were cleaned, clothes pressed and packed, we bathed and had our long hair washed and brushed, with Grandmother supervising operations. Mother was busy filling the biscuit tins for her absence and baking large batches of bread and buns. Next morning we set off early, packed into the little Ford, and away we chugged up the Hill, Mother confident at the wheel, all waving expansively. It was sad to leave Father but he had Grandmother and perhaps one of the aunts to care for him.

We always carried such necessities for the journey as food, a billy, a spade and an axe. The road took us past Matawai, uphill and downhill over the tortuous folds of the Raukumara Ranges, with a last great climb over Otoko Hill. Eighty kilometres separated us from our destination and the road was primitive, with steep grades and sticky clay patches in the valleys, all of which tested a car and its driver to the utmost. And at this time of the year the water in the dreaded creek crossings (and there were about eight to negotiate) usually ran high with the spring rains. Most we managed to cross successfully with the aid of a sack over the radiator and, of course, the high chassis of the Ford helped. But if the electrical part of the engine became damp, the car stalled and refused to restart and we simply had to wait for it to dry out, with the car bonnet temporarily removed. Also, there was the danger that the impact of the huge boulders submerged under the rushing brown torrent would damage the chassis. Sometimes several cars would be gathered at the worst fords as the problems of crossing were shared. Sometimes it was decided to wait an hour or two for the water to subside which it did fairly quickly if there had been only a shower, and at these times we brought out our picnic lunch. Provisions for several meals were always carried. As a last resort, if it were getting late, or the current very swift, a car could be hitched to a nearby log or fence strainer by a cable of No. 8 wire to sustain it against the current, which operation required the cooperation of someone to ease the slack with a wire strainer as the car progressed. Mother, as a lone woman driver, was always helped with alacrity on such occasions.

I remember once, when it was beginning to get late, Mother decided to risk it at the last crossing, the dreaded Mahaki, at the foot of the Otoko Hill. As we entered the swift current, the water rose steadily through the floorboards of the car and (terrible thought), it began to soak into our beloved gramophone which we were taking into town for repairs. We retrieved the gramophone from the floor, lifted our feet and tucked them under us and shut our eyes to the swiftly rushing water outside. Mother was too busy with the car to notice, as it lurched and bumped over the boulders, and next thing we were safely over and her deft handling of the car was praised by the onlookers. The thing was to keep it moving at an even pace if possible. Then the next car 'took the water', and others followed, helped by the wire.

Further down the road another awful emergency occurred. We were now safely over the hills, but there still remained the long and tricky road-and-rail bridge at Waikohu. By now it was just dusk, and as Mother liked to arrive in daylight if at all possible, she was hurrying the little car along. We were half-way over the long and bumpy bridge, with its two raised planks to enable the car wheels to straddle the train rails. I'll never forget the moment of sheer terror which we all experienced when we realized that the glaring red eye suddenly confronting us through the dim twilight ahead was the headlamp of the approaching train, rounding the corner of the steep slope towards the other side of the bridge. Mother, grim-lipped and quick-thinking, in a moment of desperate choice, pushed down the accelerator, and we rushed towards the train, the little car bucking on the rails. We slid off the bridge on to the road seconds before the monster crashed by with a thunderous noise. The engine-driver probably never saw us. Mother stopped the car, shaken to the core, and we all got out for a while. The 'Riverford' folk were horrified to hear of this narrow escape and our welcome was especially warm that night.

The holidays always flew by and other cousins were usually staying, making a large family party. Many and original were our exploits in these beloved surroundings. We went sliding on the heads of foliage cut from the native cabbage trees which grew everywhere, down the steep hills, their clay surfaces spring-damp and soft. We attained an exhilarating speed on our leafy toboggans, but were often catapulted off at the bumps formed by the horizontal sheep tracks round the hillsides and we got covered with papa mud in the process. We were given small sums of spending money with which to visit the little general store at Ormond where we dithered delightedly over a choice of bubble gum or sticky changing balls. On Sundays, ceremonial visits were paid to the little hill cemetery, surrounded by old trees, where many of our elders are buried. It is still there today, little changed. We loved the small white turnstile gates, and at the summit we would look with delight over the far view. Greenness of every tone, of hedges, willows, fields, soothed the eye; a patch of ploughed beige, a glimpse of a large country house gleaming white against a gentle billow of trees on the slope beyond; everywhere a rounded softness of land contour slowly expanding through the sunny haze to the deep dull blue of the distant ranges. Somewhere away over there lay our Gorge . . . Then we would turn our interest to the craggy old tombstones. Many were our questions and mother was always (to us) intolerably sad over the little grave of her first-born, planted with white roses, now budding. Buoyant feelings were frowned on by the grown-ups and, on the whole, we were glad when the afternoon was over.

One day, being momentarily bored by the usual occupations, we concocted a desperate plan, led by Cousin Tom, the eldest of the group. He and Cousin Timmy solemnly issued a dare to each of the rest of the group to stay under the nearby cattle-stop when the train passed over it. The train, of course, always held hypnotic fascination for us when it passed through the little village station twice daily. We four older children accepted the dare and duly squeezed under the space at the side of the railway, crouching in the pit beneath, close to the appointed time. Soon we could hear the distant throbbing of the approaching train. I'm sure we were all quite panic-stricken but it was too late to get out. So we huddled up closer together with our heads down and our hands over our ears, the smell of the damp earth in our nostrils. Suddenly IT was upon us and the roaring and clanging were deafening and calamitous. The ground shook and we felt mortally sick. When it was all over, we crept out to meet the scared white faces of the younger ones. Never, *never*, again . . . But next day we were bragging about it. Until Cousin Tom said slowly, 'It *might* have let out some hot water on us . . .' and the subject was forever dropped.

Milder pursuits were playing cowboys and Indians amongst the thick garden shrubbery with its bamboo clumps entwined by smilax, or digging a cave in a soft clay bank. A rather decorous life was lived in the old homestead and there were many helpers as the aunts stayed with the family until marriage. It had gracious wide verandahs, a long hall dimly lit by coloured glass door panels, with one corner devoted to a collection of Maori artifacts: spears and stone axe heads. The large drawing-room with its quiet, rather prim atmosphere, contained a big bay window festooned with pot plants behind a hand-carved panel. There were two pianos, one a tinkly old one, very tall, with a ruby embroidered velvet front panel and beautifully wrought woodwork in twisted rosewood; the other, a more modern one on which the aunts played and accompanied songs. Here sedate afternoon teas were held with neighbours and friends calling to partake of fresh scones, cucumber sandwiches and dainty cakes. We were duly presented, washed and brushed. 'Waioeka' Grandmother had seen to our manners and, although considered to be from the bush, we were looked upon with cordiality by the visitors.

In the evenings we arranged concerts in the drawing-room, for 'Riverford' Grandma and the aunts, singing the songs of the First World War which Mother had taught us, and reciting our school poems. 'Riverford' Grandma was a quiet philosophical person and a gentlewoman. She read us stories round the fire. 'Now, wait a bit . . . wait a bit', she would say gently to our sometimes impetuous questions and requests. At times we roasted chestnuts in the big fireplace as we listened to stories about our maternal uncles in their youth, when we decided that, perhaps, we weren't so bad after all . . . although we never told anyone about the cattle-stop. We heard reminiscences of Mother's girlhood: of tennis, swimming, and riding parties, portraying a world quite foreign to us.

The highlight of the spring season was 'The Show', the annual function of the local Agricultural and Pastoral Society, where all the local families and those from the remote hinterland met up for the day and exchanged greetings and news over picnic luncheons. Mother had spent much time during the winter sewing for us girls our show frocks. They were made of crisp floral cottons (Britway cloth), flounced, and bound with matching braid. We loved the new smell of the material and they were tangible tokens, through the dark days of winter, of the approach of the Show. We touched and handled them lovingly. When the day came we felt most important in them and our joy in the day was heightened. Mother never missed making a new frock for each of us for the Show on her old Singer treadle-machine and she never used patterns.

For us children, the sideshows and merry-go-rounds were the highlights of the Show. Haunted by sheer delight, we eagerly absorbed the smell of freshly trampled grass, of sawdust, of freshly cooked hot dogs and pop-corn, and the riot of colour and action . . . We loved watching the speed and grace of the horses as they wheeled and jumped through their paces, and were terribly proud that mother had once been a Show rider. Our uncles always bought us candy-floss, great cones of melting pink stickiness, and Kewpie dolls on sticks dressed in circular gathered silk skirts in brilliant colours – lime green frosted with silver, deep blue checked in gold. The live monkeys attracted us most but I remember a sideshow in which a scantily dressed lady with improbably red cupid lips posed in various attitudes: 'Prayer', 'The Dancer', etc. I think I admired her greatly, and told Grandmother all about it. She became very upset. 'Dreadful sideshow people! Don't let them go again, Ivy (to Mother). No good will come of it.' At which my spirits fell indeed.

Once I unwittingly slipped out of the shallow swing seat of a merry-go-round swinging around at its fastest pace, and hung dangling by the arms in space, being terrifyingly whirled around. Poor Mother, quite unable to attract the attention of the attendant in charge who vacantly gazed about him, bored to distraction, could only stand by in agony and cry as encouragingly as she could 'Hang on Judy!' as I appeared with each hectic revolution and the gramophone blared on. At last, the driver realized something was amiss by the shouts from the agitated knot of onlookers, and brought the contraption to a grinding halt, just as I was beginning to despair and feel frightfully dizzy . . . I was told I was very brave and led away to have some more candy-floss and ice-cream.

Town visits held many impressions to be stored for months after our return to the hills. The town smell of the streets and shops, the important clip-clop of the baker's horses as the van wove among the traffic on the bitumen streets, bananas and oranges, new dolls which (what heaven!) we were allowed to choose, the beautiful complexions of their china faces, their hair a soft brown cloud, their dresses of crisp gingham.

Inevitably the time came to depart and, once again, we piled into the little Ford. Regret always possessed us, and the embraces of the aunts were warm. Goodbye to the lovely broad river and the poplars, goodbye to the railway tunnel and its dear little hill, goodbye Tom and Timmy and the others. By the time we neared home after the usual hazards of the journey we were asleep. Next day our beloved pets absorbed our interest, and it was good to see Father and Grandmother again. But we always had the feeling of being closed in by the mountains — even the light seemed different.

However, spring had come to the Gorge, too. The apples and the old quince were in blossom, and the whiu-whiu-whiu of the wood pigeons as they flapped across from the bush-clad slope to the pines near the homestead was frequent. And now, there was the distinctive sound of quail calling, heard only in the spring . . . Mother looked out our summer clothes for the warmer days and we revelled in the freedom of having bare arms and feet again. Christmas and summer would soon be here.

7

Summer

Summer was our season. Everywhere about us there was water and the plashing of the creeks was a sound ever present. In summer the water brought a special pleasure. From daylight till dark we explored the myriad branches of the creeks singing and flowing swiftly over their stony beds, interrupted by many bubbling little waterfalls as they made their rapid descent to the main streams. Time meant nothing to us. We would spend a whole morning building a dam, painstakingly heaving boulders into place to form a wide base, then building them upwards and filling the chinks in with smaller stones and shingle. Beneath the dam the water seethed away in shallow frustration, as if angry at our attempts to hold it up.

These dams were surprisingly effective in deepening the pool we had chosen as the summer's swimming place. As the water above the dam rose first to our knees, then to our thighs, and finally over waist-depth at the base of the waterfall which fed the pool, so did our sense of achievement soar. Cousins always stayed with us in the summer holidays and so there were perhaps eight children of all ages, a force which could achieve amazing results on a chosen project. Of course, at the first fresh in the creek, our hard-won dam would be swept away, but meanwhile we had a pool deep enough for us to learn to float and to practise some tentative swimming strokes. Afterwards we would lie and dream in a patch of soft yellow-flowered clover on the edge of the creek, our bareness blissfully fanned by a warm wind. When alone, we girls dispensed with our bathing things, but not without a bothersome thought or two about Grandmother's reaction, should she hear of it!

On other days we rolled large logs or boulders down the steep hill faces for the sheer thrill of the effort involved in pushing and heaving them into momentum and watching them tremble, then tumble, slowly, then faster and faster, until they leapt end over end down a steep slope into the creek bed below, to land with a satisfying whump and crash, and perhaps break to pieces on the rocks.

The summer of 1931 was very hot and we played constantly in the creeks. As usual, the aunts and various cousins were staying, and some of us slept in Grandmother's cottage. One warm night, Gael and I went to bed as usual in the large brass double bedstead, and soon we slept soundly. But at about 2 a.m. we were suddenly awakened by the rattling of the cottage windows and the heaving of the bed. Aunt Jane came rushing in, in the thick darkness, to calm us as the brass bedheads tinkled and shook. It was an earthquake, she said. The shaking was soon over and, wonderingly, we went to sleep again.

Some weeks later, on a hot February morning, we children were all off again as usual up the creeks. But the morning was sultry, and somehow our dam-building seemed to pall suddenly. We drifted back to the orchard in search of inspiration. Here, there was an old ivy-covered outhouse, now disused, as Father had set up less primitive sanitation arrangements nearer the houses. Its dark interior was thick with cobwebs, and somehow it fascinated us. Cousin Tom, always a leader, dared Larry and me to be shut in the spidery dark, in turns. Of course, if one declined a dare, one's prestige with the group fell noticeably and one could be ignored for the rest of the day, or taunted by cowardly nicknames. And so, in turns, Larry and I braved the dark mustiness and the yawning pit in the interior, gritting our teeth. When the claustrophobia became unbearable we would shout 'Come on, so-and-so, it's your turn now', and were terribly relieved to see the daylight again. Cousin Tom seemed rather reluctant but, barracked by us all, in he went. And just as we had firmly latched the door from the outside, a frightful commotion fell upon us. The whole valley commenced to rock and heave. The old orchard trees seemed to bend nearly to the ground. Around some of the surrounding hills where the bush hid steep slopes formed by towering masses of loose rock, boulders were crashing down into the creek beds, and the noise was deafening. In one concerted terrified rush, we took to our heels towards the house where we were met by the agitated grown-ups who hastily counted us. 'Where's Tom?' they cried. Heavens! we'd left him locked up. And pitiful howls coming from the direction of the orchard testified to his agony, as Larry rushed back to rescue him. Soon all was calm again, but during the day small tremors kept occurring and we were confined to the house and garden. And, for once, we were quite willing to stay there. Grandmother insisted on special prayers said together before we all retired to face the night.

Later, we read and heard of the terrible loss of life and damage in Napier on the coast 320 kilometres south-east of the Gorge. Earthquakes were our favourite topic of conversation for months afterwards. And we never realized just how lucky we were that we were not in one of our usual haunts in those critical minutes as falling rocks from the slopes were a deadly danger.

Soon we were back eeling in the creeks again. All six of us hunted the small black eels which were to be found under the rocks. We would work our way up a chosen stretch of the creek, leaving no likely stone unturned, as quickly and quietly as possible, eyes glued to the water. Then, suddenly, there was an electric flicker of a tail in the bright sunlight; we scooped up the eel with our hands and flung it, wriggling madly, out on to the bank where the boys quickly despatched it by a blow on its head with a stone. Sometimes when the eel escaped to another rock, Tom or Larry ordered a plan of campaign, each child being assigned to a position by a rock where the eel might choose to hide. Skill and rapid movement of hand and eye were at a premium and sometimes the eels would seem to disappear into nowhere. The trophies were strung on a poplar stick to be skinned on our return home. Mother was always good-natured about frying them for us and the flesh was delicate, white and tasty, though sparse.

Another eeling method was to use a gaff, a fish-hook mounted on the end of a large stout stick, to quickly hook an eel from a pool. The elders always warned us about the dangers of these, and we only used gaffs as a last resort. But one day, the boys had baled up a big one in a pool in the larger creek which ran along below the road bank not far from the house. Cousin Timmy had a gaff and was determined to get the eel. All at once the eel flashed out over the rocks at the edge of the pool. Timmy swiped at it. The gaff flew backwards, and Timmy overbalanced. Then disaster fell. In the confusion, Timmy stepped on the gaff and the big hook entered the

sole of his foot irretrievably. In desperation, someone was despatched to the house for help, and we knew we were for it, besides
being terribly concerned on Timmy's behalf. Mother hurried
down, calm, but very anxious. She found her worst fears realized.
Timmy was in great pain, and our faces were glum. Mother didn't
scold us much, to our relief.

As the creek was near the road, a passing driver noticed the
distress of the party and stopped. With the help of this kindly
motorist, it was decided to file the hook from the gaff, thus sepa-
rating Timmy from the cumbrous stick. He was taken home in the
car, and hobbled inside, as bravely as he could. Poor Mother! What
a conundrum she had upon her hands. We were all those miles
from a doctor and the danger from dreaded blood poisoning was
uppermost in her mind. Sister Pritchard, the District Nurse whose
name was a household word, was summoned from Matawai and
arrived as quickly as possible in her sturdy car. Meanwhile, Timmy
was given an aspirin and made to rest with his foot on a pillow.
Sister arrived and surveyed the situation dispassionately. We were
all terribly worried and we huddled about outside the porch where
Timmy lay, silently sympathizing. Sister sent us packing. The full
import hit us shockingly when we heard poor Timmy's awful
screams. We fled up the creek, out of earshot, unable to bear it any
longer. When we returned, white and utterly miserable, it was to
find Timmy asleep. Sister was a woman of action and she extricated
the fish-hook, the barb of which was deeply buried but with the
shank protruding. By pushing the curved shank through a half-
circle in the soft tissue of the foot she was able to grasp the barb
firmly as it emerged, and extract the hook. There was little pain
relief in those days and Timmy went through untold suffering.
Sister, too, had been terrified of blood poisoning as a result of the
long delay of getting him to hospital and her action probably saved
Timmy's leg. Timmy was highly praised by everyone for his pluck-
iness. But we never forgot the agony of that day. And gaffs were
forever banned.

8

The Depression

By now the harsh realities of the deteriorating economic situation were being felt throughout New Zealand, especially in family life. Our isolation from the cities and villages meant that, mercifully, we did not experience the bitter inequalities and comparisons which affected neighbourhood groups elsewhere. Thus we were not really conscious of any deprivation as individuals.

But we children began to sense a growing anxiety on the part of the adults. There was a great deal of discussion among them which dwindled to silence in our presence. One day, we heard Grandmother declaiming to Father, 'They can *turn* us out. We'll live under an umbrella before they move us from the land!' We worried about the ominous 'they'. Whoever would want to turn us out? There was also much discussion about the farm stock and what should be done with it. Sheep and cattle were by now unsaleable commodities and on many farms they were being slaughtered and burnt as farmers were unable to feed them and could not afford to shear them.

Another day, I came across a pile of unpaid bills in Father's desk each besprinkled with peremptory demands for payment and I felt desperately worried. The only thing I could think of to do was to make him a little box for his desk for paper clips and so on, in the hope that this would comfort him, while feeling bitterly at the same time its futility. Into the making of the box went much anxious care and concern.

Then the tension seemed to ease a little. Apparently a decision had been made. Father was to enlarge the slaughterhouse, kill the stock and sell the meat in the nearest town, Opotiki, at the coast end of the Gorge. By now, our Ford had been worn out and exchanged for an Essex, with a light van-type body for carrying general farm supplies. Meanwhile, Mother, with almost superhuman patience, had taught Father to drive on the Gorge road, although he was not an expert as yet. We watched Father and Cousin Stewart carefully concrete the slaughterhouse floor and line it with galvanized flat-iron, fitting it with heavier pulleys and equipment.

Here, cattle and sheep were to be slaughtered and prepared for market, and the internal parts – liver, tripe, heart, kidneys, sweetbreads and brains – were carefully and thoroughly washed in the creek water nearby, ice-cold in winter. We learnt much in the slaughterhouse about animal biology and were interested and intensely curious, but still could never bring ourselves to eat the snowy white tripe. Although we were always banished from the shooting of the cattle, we managed to stay within earshot and always felt a curious mixture of awe, excitement, and deep regret for the animal. Mother assured us that the cattle did not feel much and that they had had a good life on the hills, but we felt it a terrible thing for anything to thus be bailed up and shot.

Apparently the thought of entering 'Trade' had appalled Grandmother and Mother whose people had farmed for generations. But Grandmother, especially, hated waste and debts to others. 'Anyway,' she said, 'Humphrey de T. had to do it in adverse circumstances.' Humphrey was a son of the noble English family from whom we humble colonials were descended on Grandfather's side, I learnt later. The 'adverse circumstances' occurred through the said Humphrey being turned out by his baron father for some youthful peccadillo, whereupon he opened a butcher's shop in the local village. A rather different case from the hard necessity which was the family's now.

And so the little Essex set out twice a week, loaded with meat, on its journey through the perilous Gorge. Father was lucky if he was able to return the same night, for though the distance was only fifty-eight kilometres, the travelling was slow and arduous. He soon found that conditions amongst the Opotiki families were heart-rending as many were quietly starving. Therefore he sold what meat he could and gave the rest away, not forgetting the gangers still working on the lower reaches of the road. Many people were helped in this way, and they paid him back in whatever kind they could: fresh vegetables, fruit or shop stock. The strain fell heavily upon Mother and Grandmother, and many a night they sat up by candle-light waiting for the little van to return in the early hours of the morning, Grandmother reading her Bible and praying.

The worst time occurred during one Christmas season. We children had been preparing for the festivity for days, as had the grown-ups. We carried home bundles of fern fronds and the spires of pink and white foxgloves, which grew in masses in the small gullies. With these we lined the porch walls where the dinner table was to be set. We filled all the house vases with roses, and the newly-clayed fireplaces with large jars containing branches of sweet-smelling mauve buddleia. The grown-ups prepared cooked ham, poultry, plum puddings and Christmas cake, omitting some of the dried fruit as it was now a luxury. Grandmother baked her special Lincolnshire Melton Mowbray raised pork pies (round-walled with soft lard pastry) which she had learned to make for Grandfather, and fruit mincemeat pies, another specialty of hers.

Father decided to go to Opotiki the day before Christmas Day with a load of meat and return with some extras for us such as sticks of striped rock-candy, maybe a pineapple or coconut, and small items for the stockings, not forgetting Mother, Grandma, and the aunts. To this end, Aunt Jane and Cousin Helen, both young nurses on holiday at the farm, accompanied him. Christmas Eve came and we went to bed happy and expectant now that the great day was nearly here. We knew, too, that a large bulky parcel addressed in Aunts Nan's upright hand had arrived recently in the mail, and also one from Aunt Ella, another favourite adult. Of course, since going to school, we were quite aware of the origin of Santa Claus and Mother had said we must think of him as the 'Spirit of Xmas', of jollity, love, and the cheering of others. And now Aunt Nan was with us in person to add to our delight.

Early dawn, with its soft summer mist and promise of a golden day was always beautiful on fine days in the Gorge. And it brought the usual intensity of excitement as we explored our stockings.

'What have you got, Larry? O-oh, look, I've got water-wings.'

'Hope I can borrow them?' from Larry, for once respectful.

'O-oh, look, I've got a scented soap bunny. Smell it! And water-flowers. Gee, just what I wanted!'

We rushed in to share the treasures with our parents, and then the blow fell. WHERE was father? Mother, sitting up alone in bed, could not conceal her anxiety from us, though she comforted us as best she could, saying that they had probably decided to stay the night in Opotiki. But she kept going to the telephone. This old-fashioned instrument connected the family with the settlers in the lower reaches of the Gorge by a flimsy line strung from tree trunk to tree trunk. Mother hoped to ascertain whether any of the neighbours had seen or heard the little van pass during the night. Between the last reaches of the Gorge and Opotiki, there was no telephone link at all, nor is there today. As a result, she could not find out whether they had set out, but we knew she felt sure they had, and that something had happened. Mother nearly always knew when any of the family were ill or in danger; and Grandmother, too, had strong intuition, or as it may be said was Fey, as of course are many Scots.

Under the circumstances, our presents were of little comfort as we knew too much about that Gorge road. Aunt Nan did her best to divert us and suggested that we show our presents to Grandma. We did, but the joy had gone. And Grandmother was reading her Bible. After an age of desolation, the telephone rang at last. It was a neighbour about sixteen kilometres distant, who broke the news as gently as possible. The van had gone over into the river and fallen about twenty metres, but miraculously the occupants were alive and comparatively unhurt, although shocked and badly cut and bruised. Cousin Helen, a sturdy girl, had suffered some deep cuts about the face. They were all resting in bed at the neighbour's home and arrangements were being made to take the girls to hospital. Father had managed to scramble up the side of the Gorge, an almost superhuman feat in the darkness, and go for help. He was now able to return to us. We listened horror-struck, but deeply thankful. It brought to me personally the first real sense of a Something behind the visible realities; 'The Watchful Mind of God', Grandmother said. Poor Mother and Aunt Nan, who had been so calm and brave, now wept freely and then as quickly became calm again. We had our Christmas but the mood was sober and thankful, and poor Father, when he at last appeared, looked terribly white.

Apparently, Father had stopped in dense darkness to help a fellow traveller whose car had broken down. Father parked the van on the narrow road verge. They had got the other car started again and in moving off, handicapped by the inferior headlamps of those days, Father had misjudged the nearness of the edge and the van had slipped over, to plunge terrifyingly to the river below. The little car was quite wrecked and was later hauled to the surface to be used for spare parts. Somehow, Father had climbed an almost sheer rock face of twenty metres, in pitch darkness, safely.

Father was to have two more similar experiences and emerge unscathed, whereas a dear old couple, who were learning to drive their car, went over and were both killed instantly as the car struck the rocky riverbed. Another tragedy occurred when one of our young teachers was killed. His motor cycle failed to take a sharp bend and shot out into space to crash into the stream below. Such was the constant toll of the Gorge road.

The depression years dragged on. The family now economized to the limit. As little butter as possible was used, as butter could be sold. Porridge with milk was plentiful. Our meat often consisted of stuffed sheeps' hearts, lambs fry with a little bacon, tripe or sweet-breads, as the joints of the meat could be sold more readily. Mother made wonderful barley soups and oxtail stews. The grown-ups contrived generally to produce apparel and furnishings from older and used materials. Sandshoes became our main footwear, and much homespun knitting was done. We were never short of food and grew up very robust, except for our teeth which were always troublesome. There were many people worse off than us who visited our door for food and lodging and were never refused. Many of them were well educated, sensitive and perceptive individuals, each with a personal tragedy in their immediate past.

The state of our teeth necessitated visits to a dentist in Opotiki when crises arose and after vinegar, a smidgeon of brandy, or 'Painkiller' – a proprietary remedy stocked by a travelling salesman – had failed to allay the cruel aching. Usually, extractions were necessary. We travelled to Opotiki on the service-car, finding our own way to the dentist's rooms from the depot. It was a huge adventure, except for the teeth part; although the dentist was a kindly man, the dental administrations of the time were fairly primitive. That dreadful, dreadful, treadle drill! His assistant, a plump motherly Irish girl, was wonderful to us, as were the service-car passengers on the return journey as they eyed our tearfulness and swollen cheeks, and plied us with sweets.

The family kept in close touch with nearby connections. Aunt Eva, from Te Araroa on the Cape, sometimes came to stay bringing some of her large family to visit Grandmother, and to help. She lived in this isolated pioneer East Coast settlement where she was the district nurse and much of her life was spent in looking after the neighbourhood people, the majority being Maori. She regarded this service as an extension of her role as mother to her own large family of eight children. When she stayed, we children helped to nurse and sing to her current baby, and learnt much from her. Aunt Eva was a wonderfully comforting personality, with a simple kindly philosophy, and though she had the same piercing blue eyes as Grandmother, she was never sharp with her tongue.

Aunt Ella, Mother's sister, always called for a night or two on her way to Ruatoki where she was stationed at the Anglican Maori Mission and she too told us of Maori ways and customs, and her life at Ruatoki, also in the Urewera. Cousin Gordon, another relative of Scots extraction and a school teacher, called on his way to Gisborne in his smart red convertible sports car and always played the bagpipes to us. This was a memorable experience, to hear the pipes skirling, the reedy notes echoing up the valleys just as they had done in Scotland of old.

It struck us that Cousin Gordon did not believe in soft ways with children and we imagined him being very fierce with his school class when his patience was tried and he fixed them with a glare. He had bushy eyebrows and a balding dome and was the colonial equivalent of the Scottish dominie (schoolmaster). But with us he was all affability and twinkle. We came to like him and his music held sheer enchantment, which he well knew. Aunt Bea and Tom and Timmy, with whom we had long played in 'Riverford' holidays, arrived from the city for a prolonged stay. They were a welcome addition to our household as Aunt Bea was a most cheerful, amusing person and the two boys had always been regarded as extra brothers. Cousin Tom was slightly older than I and became our leader.

I took this with as much grace as I could, but I well remember feeling that I had to prove that I, as a girl, could go it alone and emerge victorious from the hurly burly of 'King I Seen Ee', a kind of extended scrum, where all combined to hurl the runner down as he or she tried to traverse the length of a field against the pack, using speed, skill, dodging and wit. Another incident in which the males seemed to be maddeningly unjust, stuck in my memory. We were to be photographed at 'Riverford' one holidays and the current litter of puppies was scooped up from their kennel, for accessories in the snap. As our group was comprised of four children and there were four puppies, their equal distribution seemed assured. But no! To my astonishment and rage, Tom and Timmy held two puppies each while Gael (happily unaware because too young) and I were left pupless! I sulked darkly in the background and refused to stand with the boys. Somehow that injustice lodged itself in my subconscious, and is probably still there.

By now, many of the soldier settlers in the Gorge were moving out, as the financial struggle was lost and the ever-encroaching fern moved in. Mortgages became crippling. The farmers were unable to buy wire, staples and essential materials. This was the beginning of the end of the Gorge country as farm land. At last, in about 1935, a mortgage commission was appointed by the government of the day to adjust the large debts owed by most remaining farmers, all over New Zealand, to their stock firms. Father went to Court to state his case, in the hope of obtaining some help in restarting farming operations. But to everyone's astonishment, it was disclosed that, as a result of his efforts with the butchering business, the stock firm owed *him* a small sum and no help was deemed necessary. The Commissioner, a dry personality, merely said to the firm's representative, 'I suggest you shout your client a new suit. He looks as though he needs one!'

Father returned, proud, but bitterly disappointed, 'we should have let the b— mortgage rip. *We* were the *mugs!*' was his trenchant summary, which we overheard. It meant that we had a farm which had slipped back to a large degree and no capital to rebuild it. The stock firms had no faith in the Gorge land now, and only two or three settlers remained. Father never really recovered his interest in 'Raysburn' as a farm again, and this influenced his later decision to move to the flats and to enter local body politics. He developed a very non-conformist outlook. (One of the causes dear to his heart, in later life was the rehabilitation of service personnel from World War II. He was awarded the signal honour of the Returned Services Association's Gold Cross for his work.) The indignation of Grandmother and Mother over this affair of the commission was unbridled and vocal. But we had all survived The Depression, and were healthy, which was the main thing, however uncertain the future.

9

Milestones

One autumn as we were nearing the May holidays, it was announced that Cousin Minna, an elderly relative, was to help Grandma while Mother had a holiday. This was quite inexplicable to us, as didn't we always go *with* her on holidays? Mother certainly hadn't seemed her usual jolly self lately. We began to gloom about the possibility that she was suffering from some incurable disease, and that we were not being told. We became very restive, and were at times openly resentful towards the grown-ups. We questioned old Cousin Stewart, but got very evasive replies.

Mother, seeing all this, at last told us the reason. And we were utterly surprised. She was to have a baby! She told us in a careful talk, very tactfully and quietly, about the facts of birth. We were quite impatient, as of course we *knew* all *this*. But what did she think it would be? Larry wanted a boy and I a girl, and we became quite fierce on the point. I was allowed to sew some baby clothes, which I felt to be a great privilege. Of course we announced our big news at School and were temporarily the envy of them all. Then the elder school girls began to tell us in insidious whispers in the playground of all the things which could go wrong. We tried steadfastly not to think of what they had said. We had never thought of there being danger to Mother. But they persisted that they knew a lady who like Mother was not very young who had . . . . Then they began to 'feel sorry' for us, at which we were furious.

When Mother duly departed, we were very downcast and poor Aunt Minna, who was staid and prim, had a hard time of it. Sometimes we felt that the worry of it all was just too much to bear. There was inevitably antagonism between Aunt Minna and us; I think she was glad to see us off to school in the morning each day. One extremely wet cold June day, when we came home from school in the afternoon, she had news for us. We had a baby brother and

Mother was well! We immediately forgave poor Aunt for her supposed trespasses, and we couldn't wait to tell the other school children. They were very envious and hoped they would be able to see the baby soon. We said we would have to see. Then the great day came. After school, we rushed across the log bridge from the service-car, not really believing that Mother would be home. But she was, and there on the settee, all wrapped in a cobweb-fine Shetland wool shawl sent by our Scottish Aunt, was the most beautiful tiny baby we had ever hoped to see. Once again, it was almost too much.

Nursing the baby was squabbled over, and in the ensuing days, fetching and carrying for him was our chief occupation after school hours. But Mother was far from well for a time, for the long strain of the depression had drained her resources. Sometimes, as the eldest, I was desperately worried. But the trouble passed and soon it was summer. In no time young Gordon was able to toddle and we took him everywhere about the homestead environs, one of us on either side, holding a hand. It was good to come home after one of our expeditions further afield to play with him in carefree joy. And Mother took time off from the house, to come for walks with all of us, while we took turns carrying Gordon. This was a very happy period and Mother, as her health improved, seemed to blossom. Her 'little afterthought', as she called him, was definitely a great success with the family. And Grandmother, who was growing more frail, adored him.

Financially, things were at last improving with the guaranteed price for farm products now decreed by the government. We were to have several more happy years in the Gorge. To our further delight, Cousins Tom and Timmy gained a baby brother as well, and young Andrew and Gordon were later to become fast friends, and to spend many holidays together in the Gorge.

Now something very interesting occurred, regarding our Aunt Jane. She seemed particularly happy and jolly with us when she returned to the farm one holidays, and soon the secret was out. She had become engaged to a young farmer, a son of an old Bay family. Everyone was very happy for her, especially Grandmother. One day as I ran into the cottage unexpectedly, I surprised Grandmother as she admired Jane's beautiful ring, trying it on her finger, and turning it this way and that to catch the light. Grandmother had a weakness for beautiful jewellery which she probably despised in herself, for after all these were 'things of the world'. Upon my appearance, she hastily put the ring away in its velvet case. I was so hoping she would let me try it on.

Much discussion about the wedding now took place. It was decided that it could be held in the 'Raysburn' homestead garden. Jane and her fiancé seemed happy about this and so plans were made and preparations went forward with a will. Entertaining crowds of guests never worried Mother, as she had sometimes had to produce dinner for a large number at short notice such as at the time that a deputation with a Minister of the Crown arrived to inspect the road works.

The house was given an especially thorough spring cleaning. As the day drew near the household silver and brass pieces were polished to a nicety, windows and floors shone, and the porches were scrubbed to an irreproachable whiteness. The flower garden was clipped and trimmed and fresh gravel from the creeks was laid upon the paths. Even father helped here (flower gardening was an unusual occupation for him). It was arranged that Reverend Salt, a minister from Opotiki much approved by Grandmother, should perform the ceremony. We children asked many questions about weddings, and being told of the custom of throwing confetti, rice, or sometimes rose petals, at the bridal pair, we began to put by a hoard of the last, drying them surreptitiously on boards in one of the sheds. We were also put upon our honour to behave ourselves well.

Summer was in full bloom. The day arrived and was perfect. The deutzia shrub was a flowering mass of bridal white tassels and roses flung perfume everywhere. Masses of dark red spice-scented sweet-william stood in the garden borders. A marquee was erected on the lawn and food was laid out upon the tables from early morning onwards. Wild sucking pigs, ham, colonial goose, poultry, trifles laden with cream and made with our own fresh raspberries, home-made ale and a quantity of wine and stronger spirits, comprised the fare. Grandmother had baked a large wedding cake. We girls were dressed in our best red and blue velvet frocks, with short sleeves and cream lace collars which Mother had made. Representatives

from the whole of Father's family, with its many branches, attended, some arriving from far distant districts of the Bay and beyond,
and many stayed the night before or after the wedding. We children
were highly delighted and excited by the presence of so many
visitors. We were duly presented by father to Great-uncle David
Cameron from 'Toroa' on the Gisborne plain, who was Grandmother's brother and originally from Southland. He was a tall man
with a large reddish moustache who laughed and talked a lot, but
who was very dignified withal. He patted us on our heads, and said
that we were nice-looking children, and that we would be a credit
to the clan. At which we giggled with embarrassment. Everyone
seemed to defer to him, and he was known as a great scholar of the
Bible and a kindly man. He was the head of the family, we realized
later, and even Father treated him with much respect. Though we
rather liked him, we were glad to escape his presence.

We liked our future uncle, and the kindliness of his quiet character. But we were determined to enter into the spirit of things by
throwing our rose petals at him at the appropriate time. At last the
bride appeared, looking slim and pretty in her flounced white silk
taffeta, her deep auburn hair graced by an exquisitely beautiful old
lace veil, a Cameron family heirloom made by nuns of an Irish
convent (somehow it came into the family possession from connections there).

Now a hush fell upon the gathering, and the simple ceremony
began. After it the Reverend Salt eulogized the beautiful setting,
and we were very gratified privately that our Gorge was so much
appreciated. Cousin Gordon set up on the bagpipes for the wedding procession round the lawn to the marquee, and our excitement knew no bounds. The 'March of the Cameron Men'
affected us deeply. Young Gordon, in his large play-box formed
from a tea chest, also seemed to revel in the music and everyone
spoke to him.

Wine and talk flowed freely, and at last the time came for bride
and groom to depart. We thought of our rose petals and rushed off
to get them. Alas! They seemed to be a little damp and mouldy. But
we were not to be daunted. Sorting out the best, we quickly returned and pelted them at the departing couple as they proceeded
sedately, to the music of the pipes, down the path towards the gate.

To their credit, they remained smiling and good-humoured throughout. After much kissing and embracing from all the clan, they were away, driving down the Gorge in the late afternoon sunlight. The grown-ups drifted inside the house to sit down and have a last talk together, before departure or preparations to stay the night were made.

Now, a dreadful flatness fell upon us children. The marquee looked sadly deserted but there were many interesting looking bottles, still partly full, standing on the tables. Inspiration seized us. We had never tasted wine. This was our chance. Larry and I downed a glass each. Lovely burning warm sensation in the throat and mouth! Some more was poured. And suddenly we felt very peculiar and wobbly. But what if Grandmother . . . Larry would get a severe tanning and we girls a scolding, which we felt was even harder to bear. The thought sobered us immediately and we hurriedly put down our glasses. Somehow the idea of bed beckoned strongly, and we crept in through the back porch, so as to avoid the grown-ups. The next day we were commended for our helpfulness and good behaviour (the rose petal incident tactfully forgotten), which made us feel very guilty temporarily. But we were not really sorry we had tasted our fill of that good wine.

10

Growing Up

We had had a carefree childhood, choosing our activities as the mood took us. Mother, with her gentle outlook did not believe in tying young children to a timetable, apart from that of school. But now, largely of our own accord, we began to participate in the chores and were glad to be thought of as responsible helpers. Grandmother was unstinting in her praise of our efforts.

At times, we could be unexpectedly wayward. Our school work was progressing well, and satisfactory reports came home each term from the conscientious young sole charge teacher. Eventually he decided it was time to make an attempt to get to know some of the parents. One Saturday afternoon, just as we had arrived back indoors in our usual rather tattered state, we heard a motor cycle chugging up the valley. It stopped opposite the house. We children peered out apprehensively to see Mr. P., our teacher, immaculate in well-pressed tweeds, striding purposefully across the log bridge. With startled and meaningful looks at each other, we simply took to our heels, not to reappear until the motor cycle had safely gone. Poor Mother had to make excuses for us, as Mr. P. had seen our hasty departure up the creek. Next Monday at school, we had a little lecture from him when he said that there was no need for children to run away when their teacher paid a visit to their home. He looked very dignified and rather sad, and we squirmed and felt dreadful, remembering our impulsive behaviour. Somehow to us the teacher belonged to school and that was a separate world from home. It seemed incongruous and embarrassing for the two to meet. Grandmother, too, had plenty to say about the incident. She had always been very conscious of our necessary training in the social graces. For instance, we were never allowed to answer 'Wha-a-t?' when called by her. It must always be 'Yes, Grandmother?' and so on. I'm sure this did us no harm.

A nightly freight-car service had now been instituted through the Gorge, which meant that the family was more easily able to sell perishables such as cream, butter, and eggs. And so Father bought some dozen fine Jersey cows and we elder children helped Father and Cousin Stewart with the milking. Father always did things as well as possible, and a modern little cowshed was set up, with concrete floors and drains with a plentiful supply of water from the creek. The milking was done by hand, and we took a great interest in the grades for the cream received from the factory. It was mostly 'finest' but we took it as personally insulting if it were less. We were let off milking in the mornings because of school, but after school we always fetched the cows from one of the numerous small valleys, sometimes having to hunt for them in the edges of the bush. I used to sing while wandering the valleys and developed some quite impressive top notes, not that the cows showed any appreciation. I enjoyed setting the valleys ringing with sound. We then helped with the evening milking, doing two or three cows each, which soon became our favourites.

Then at shearing, perhaps at the start of the Christmas holidays, there were many extra jobs, such as filling the sheep pens and helping with the drafting, when it was satisfying to add our chorus to the deafening noise of the dogs. We loved shearing time. Somehow it symbolized the start of summer, with golden, sunny mornings and long tranquil evenings. In the mornings we would watch with fascination as Father cranked the Lister engine in the little engine room attached to the main shed. Shooka-shooka-shooka-bang-bang Bang! Then she was away, and the wheels and pulleys of the shearing machines clacked and droned purposefully as the engine settled into a steady pace. The rhythm of it all appealed to us. We liked watching the skill of the shearers, moving smoothly through the intricate routine of shearing, always cheerful and sometimes bursting into a Maori song together as they worked. At smoko time we rushed over to the house where Mother had ready large plates of fresh scones with cream and raspberry jam, and an outsize billy of strong black tea. As the shearers relaxed, jokes flew about and snatches of talk in Maori, which we longed to understand. They taught us some words, then they would say something unintelligible (and probably ribald) to us, and laugh uproariously.

They washed themselves and their clothes in the creeks and for meals liked nothing better than a 'big mutton' or a wild pork stew, and watercress and puha (sow thistle) boiled with bacon. With their children, we collected the puha and watercress, chattering together all the while, happy at the larger clan of children.

Completing the shearing was tricky in this mountain country with its very high rainfall. Often there was a rush to get the mob under cover. If the weather was bad and the shearing delayed, the wool deteriorated quickly as the bidi-bidi burrs, from a ground plant which crept everywhere through the rough pastures, ripened and clung to the fleeces, matting them beyond repair and making them practically worthless on the wool market. So it was always a worrying time for Father.

Then came the dipping when we saddled the two old horses, Micky and Bluey, and followed the mob of sheep, two children on each horse, along the dusty road down to the Bottom Burn where a 'pot' type dip, belonging to our bachelor neighbour Mr C— was used. Here we took turns at ducking the sheep with a specially shaped crutch which neatly pushed the head of the poor animal completely under the nauseous khaki-coloured liquid for a second. This was necessary, for otherwise the pests such as lice and ticks congregated on the head and escaped. Occasionally in handling the sheep we managed to collect a tick on some part of us and were disgusted and pained, as they buried their hooks into the skin and were hard to dislodge. We felt sorry for the sheep – either way they had it hard! Then after a picnic lunch and a good feed of fat yellow wild gooseberries ripening in a spot that we knew of, we would trail home behind the mob again, enjoying the general atmosphere of action, the barking of dogs and bleating of sheep accompanied by vehement commands from Father who preferred to walk with his stick.

On hot days with perhaps a slight breeze, burning the sweet fern on the slopes was a wonderful occupation. Even Mother could sometimes be tempted to come with us, with a gleam in her eye that boded ill for the hated fern. Armed with torches made from pieces of old tyres cut and nailed onto long stout sticks then dipped into kerosene, and taking plenty of matches to light them, we toiled up the slopes. In no time, billowing white smoke clouds and burning wildly crackling fern gave us great satisfaction. We were always warned to 'keep in a line' and not to let anyone become encircled. The worst thing that ever befell us was a small burn or two on our legs from drops of melted rubber. If there was a breeze, the fern burnt with a will and a small fire would quickly become a spectacular blaze many feet high, to our great gratification.

Each spring brought the task of tracking all the goose nests, which was a challenge we looked forward to. The household flock of geese were semi-wild, and only came to be fed in the winter. They roamed the hills and valleys at will and plucked at the sweet green grass near the creeks. About September, came nesting time. The geese paired off, and a stately snow-white gander would escort his docile mate to the carefully chosen nest spot. It was always far from the homestead and cunningly concealed. They knew when we were following them and so we would pit our cunning against theirs. The gander would look at us with his small cold blue eyes and hiss a warning, his neck outstretched menacingly. Then he would cackle loudly, and the rest of the flock would answer from afar. Then the pair would commence to feed as though they had no intention whatever of going to a nest. It was as if they said, 'Whatever put that idea into your head, you silly human!' We would be exasperated, but continued to wait, patiently concealed behind a stump or below a groyne, crouched stiffly. At last, as it began to grow dark, the pair would move, quickly and directly, and, darting from cover to cover, Larry or I would follow. If they saw us the whole performance would have to be repeated. Sometimes, we lost them in the gloom and had to try again next day. But what satisfaction was ours, when at last the goose would ceremoniously and ponderously settle down on the nest, usually beneath a sheltering tree fern on the edge of the bush, where the dried fronds made ideal nesting material.

Next day, when the goose would be away again (we hoped), we would go back to investigate the number of eggs, large, brown-speckled, carefully enfolded in down and covered by dried fern or leaves. Usually there were about eight. We regularly inspected the nests, as when the first goslings hatched, the goose would proudly rejoin the flock with them, leaving perhaps four more eggs un-hatched. One or two of the eggs would be rotten, but the others contained abandoned goslings struggling to make their way out into a motherless world. These we collected carefully. Sometimes the thick shell still adhered to the tiny wriggling bundle under the white inner membrane of the egg. Without the warm moist body of the mother to provide the right conditions, they seemed to dry out. We learned never to try to remove the shell from the gosling as it was stuck fast, but to wrap it in a warm damp cloth, and leave it in the hot-water cupboard overnight, letting nature do the rest. By morning there would be an adorably fluffy greeny-yellow gosling, quite different from the revolting-looking partly hatched creature we had wrapped up the night before. Then the goslings were returned surreptitiously to the flock. Sometimes they were not accepted and we hand-reared them, feeding them patiently with moistened oatmeal. Once we took one in a basket to the Poverty Bay Agricultural and Pastoral Show and it caused a commotion among casual onlookers. One man offered to buy it, which offer we promptly refused. We always had goose for Xmas and special occasions, and sold the surplus as table birds. Each year there were some casualties as the eels had a liking for goslings and seized them as they swam in the creeks, or perhaps bit off a tiny leg, which lacerated our feelings. The slinky brown and white stoats were their predators, too.

With all the fresh-air activity we were seldom sick but we all suffered the usual spring crops of measles and mumps. Mother was wonderful at such times, feeding us up on hot milk and soups. Castor oil was the unfailing stand-by, in the opinion of the grown-ups, and I still shudder at the sight of dark blue glass bottles. From our beds we could watch the tuis and wax-eyes on the red currant blossoms outside our little bedroom window. And Mother often read to us, which was some consolation for the inactivity.

Sometimes, as a reward for our labours, Father would announce an excursion through the Gorge to the sea coast for a picnic, which produced the height of joyful anticipation. The night before we would eagerly scan the sky beyond the dark hills for signs of a fine day on the morrow. Mother baked sponge cakes and made corned beef sandwiches. Then we would be off, dressed in our best, and singing as we drove down the Gorge in the current car. Sometimes we called at The Farmers Trading Co. store in Opotiki to buy some necessities, and gazed at all the marvellous things displayed there, which somehow we knew were not for us. Then on to the beach. The first sight of the wide dark blue sea and the pale yellow sand was thrilling, glimpsed beyond the grey twisted trunks of the ancient pohutukawa trees which lined the coast. The whole day would be spent swimming and sun bathing in the hot sunshine. We would gather a sugar-bag of pipis in the shallow waves, scooping them up quickly with our hands as they attempted to burrow deeper into the sand.

One day we saw a board floating in. To our intense interest it was covered with a mass of long wriggling black stalks each with a small pipi-like shell on its head. We were told later that these were goose barnacles. We learned much about the sea coast in these trips. As the sun lowered in a classic gold and crimson sunset beyond the blue horizon, we packed up and headed homewards through the darkening Gorge, to gather round the comforting Miller lamp in the warm homestead kitchen, and tell Grandmother and Cousin Stewart all about our day. I still love the Bay of Plenty, and have a feeling of affinity with it.

11

Explorations

We grew older and more bold and, as summer came and the cousins arrived to stay, the far peaks of the horizon beckoned us. We planned and undertook many expeditions. The boys, acting the part of hardy explorers, would nonchalantly smoke dock seed 'cigarettes' while we discussed the day's activity. Of course, we girls tried them too, coughing and spluttering with the acrid fumes.

Usually we took with us matches and a substantial snack of sandwiches and apples, while good creek water was our beverage. As long as we returned by nightfall, the grown-ups appeared not to worry, though no doubt they had some misgivings at times. But it was probably hopeless to attempt to coop up such a group. As the fame of our holiday fun spread, our numbers increased. Sometimes there were as many as eighteen children staying with us. Their parents always sent up fruit and full cookie tins, while we elder children helped with the chores, such as potato peeling, picking bowls of raspberries for dessert, and washing the dishes. Poor father had to kill a sheep every second day to feed the multitude. But the family loved children, and also they liked the opportunity to widen our social experience as much as possible.

'The Waterfall' was a mecca. A swift stream tumbled over a cleft in the Top Burn country to pour down a mossy green rock face of some twenty metres into a deep foaming pool, surrounded by the narrow bushy sides of a small valley. From here it poured in a series of smaller falls, until nearer the homestead it became our docile well loved creek. We had long talked about following the creek to the falls, up the lonely valley where sometimes we saw the rare blue mountain ducks hovering in the early morning mist.

One promising summer morning we elder children set off confidently. At first we were fascinated and charmed by the beauty of the pools edged by the lovely konini and makomako and over-

hung by vivid green kidney ferns and thick mosses. The sunlight lit
the water and rocks with bright splashes, and everywhere birds
sang. The amber-shaded pools were shallow enough to wade
through and we dawdled pleasantly. But soon we came to the tough
part, where, standing in a pool, one gazed up at the almost per-
pendicular mass of rocks ahead, heaped one upon another, and
ascending steeply to the limit of our vision. We looked at one
another and our spirits almost quailed. But we were not turning
back. So up we went, clambering, slithering, hurting our toes and
finger-nails in scrabbling for holds, and too scared to look back.
Soon we could hear the deep thunder of the falls beckoning us on.
But at the head of each rocky staircase the pools were very deep. So
now we had to detour through the massed trunks of saplings in the
undergrowth at the sides of the gully, pushing and struggling
through them, panting and exhausted. After about three hours of
such effort, with many spells, we got there. And what a reward! The
waterfall was more thrilling than we could have imagined. As we
gazed at the mass of tumbling white water and sensed its weight and
power we seemed to feel ourselves drifting timelessly. The thick
cold spray was lit by a rainbow, and the fresh unique smell of bush
and water was never to be forgotten. Above all, the feeling that we
had *made it* gave us warm pleasure. Just wait till we told the grown-
ups! And so we made our way homewards, slowly but tri-
umphantly. When Aunt Nan heard about our expedition she told
us that she had been up there when she was young. Our respect for
her grew, suddenly. The challenge of the falls was always renewed;
and every summer we made our pilgrimage.

On one trip, when Larry and I were struggling along a bush
stretch, we suddenly came across a nest of little wild pigs, huddled
closely together in a hollow partly hidden by leaves and soft soil.
We thought them perfectly beautiful, and quickly picked up one
each. And of course they shrieked loudly. Then, from somewhere
behind, there came an agitated grunting and squealing in deeper
tones. The enraged sow rushed forth to do battle for her young.
'Climb a tree! Judy!' Larry yelled, as he did likewise. There we clung
to the swaying saplings just out of reach of the snapping jaws, our
hearts beating frantically. Then, praise be, the sow suddenly turned
and trotted off indignantly, followed closely by her little brood, as

she nudged them solicitiously all the while. We felt weak with fright, and fear lent us speed as we hastily quit the bush. But the experience did not deter us for long.

We explored the far ridges of the Top Burn country, toiling up the fence lines. On one occasion we saw the railway line in the far distance; although the homestead was sixteen kilometres from Matawai, on a clear frosty morning we could hear the hoot of the engine as it neared the station. And the place where the waterfall rushed over the cleft had to be explored from the top. We kept well clear of the swiftly rushing deep water as it passed through a dark piece of bush surrounding the cleft. Huge pieces of birch timber deposited by floods were caught behind the narrow opening.

Early summer mornings were wonderful for climbing, as the Gorge sun was hot on the tops at midday. And one never to be forgotten morning we had a unique experience. As always, we were walking in single file along a high ridge, while the sun was shrouded by a thick mist which also lay in the valley below us. Suddenly the sun seemed to burst through a gap. Below us, silhouetted on the opaque white mist were a row of shadows, elongated and eerie. We realised with wonder that they were ours. But the strangest thing was that each figure was surrounded by rainbow colours. It was not until years later that I heard the explanation of this, and that it is called 'The Spectre of the Brocken'. It is known in the mountain countries of Europe but is apparently rare as the combination of elements needed to produce it does not occur often. I was fascinated when I was able to identify the description of the phenomenon with this childhood experience.

Having mastered the waterfall trek, we now wanted to explore all the creeks to their sources. 'Smith's' had always been a different sort of creek. It led past the cemetery, where there grew little patches of scrub inhabited by owls, and in the spring masses of ethereal white clematis, to us the epitome of beauty and mystery. We always picked and brought it indoors, though warned against this by our Maori playmates. Some way along the valley there was a huge patch of stinging nettles, which we had encountered to our cost. The cold creek water was the best remedy, short of running home to complain which was too far anyway. Beyond this, the creek bed was unknown to us.

One afternoon, having drifted up Smith's, eeling as we went, we decided to go further, as it did not seem a very big creek. The going got tougher and we clambered over huge rocks and pushed through the thick undergrowth. But we had miscalculated the time all this exploring would take. We pushed on, unwilling to turn back. Suddenly it was six o'clock, and beginning to grow dark. At last we realized our predicament. Darkness was descending very quickly. The thought of negotiating all those tough stretches of giant rocks and thick saplings, in the pitch dark, suddenly struck us as quite impossible. We felt very despondent. Tom said, 'Anyway, we could make a nest of fern and sleep here till daylight, like the Amazon explorers.' But somehow, this didn't seem appealing, in the cold bush. 'And what about the wild pigs?' I asked. At this we thought of home and the grown-ups. They would worry! And they didn't know where we were anyway. This would probably be the end of our freedom, we thought gloomily, and inside we began to get really frightened. We thought hard and desperately. At last Tom had an idea. Far above us somewhere, in the waning light, was the road. For we knew that Smith's led past the rocky cutting. We made a sudden, unanimous decision. We would climb up onto the road and run all the way home, about two and a half kilometres. That would get us out of a scrape.

But we little knew what we were about to tackle. As we swung from sapling to sapling up the steep gully side we soon emerged out of the bush, but above us were the forbidding stretches of sheer rock face with only an occasional small tutu bush to provide hand holds. Tom, Larry, and Timmy goaded us girls on. Somehow we climbed, one by one, up the inhospitable rock, hunting for toe and hand holds, testing every step, and trying desperately not to panic or to think of the sheer drop now below us. Tom was quite curt with us girls as we were verging upon hysteria. 'You damned girls always cry. Stop booing and get on with it, or you're never coming again.' At which we became so indignant we decided to show him, which was just what he anticipated.

At last we were all safely up on the road, gazing thankfully down into the dark depths of the gully, perhaps twenty metres below us. Tom, I'm sure, was just as frightened as the rest but he had the acumen to realize that only goading would put us on our mettle.

Fear of trouble with the family lent wings to our feet as we ran homewards down the road, to us at this moment a very beautiful road. In reply to their anxious enquiries, we were very vague as to exactly where we had been. And soon we were tucking into Grandma's good dumpling stew, all our worries forgotten.

There was always the fear of our getting lost, both in the minds of the grown-ups and in ours. We knew we must always memorize the details of our surroundings as we went, and we often notched an outstanding tree or two. Then we reasoned that if we followed a creek downstream, it must bring us out to a river somewhere – not really thinking, of course, about how we would negotiate large waterfalls! This early training laid the foundations for the knowledge of the Gorge country which was to stand the boys in good stead in their later years as deerstalkers, hunters, and search and rescue personnel. Of course, for us all, it contained the elements of a wonderful training in character formation, persistence and endurance.

12

Neighbours and Legends

A couple of kilometres away, at 'The Long End', the paddock at the foot of the Hill, lived a kindly middle-aged couple. We took many walks up the road to their small cabin, which was mainly built of odds and ends from the former Public Works camp situated here. The couple always made us children feel very welcome, and pressed us to stay a little longer. The wife was a large comfortable woman and a good cook, so we enjoyed her spicy buns or a slab of rich fruit cake, with a cup of tea. The husband was tall, thin, fair, and aristocratic-looking. His passion was his violin, and he had been well taught. His instrument was a valuable one, mellow-toned, which somehow, through all the ups and downs of a varied fortune, he had managed to retain. On Saturdays, when freed from his road-keeping job, he entertained us with music in the grand manner; although we did not fully realize that hearing Dvorak's 'Humoresque' expertly played, in the little cramped cabin in the Gorge, was a unique experience.

It was a sad day for the couple when the wife fell really ill, and after some time died, tended all the while by the district nurse. Father or Mother visited poor Clive daily, and as he had only his music to console him, he began to drink more than the usual amount of whisky. But he survived to spend the rest of his life on the staff of a back country station, still playing his fiddle.

On the other side of 'Raysburn', there lived a dour bachelor farmer, who, we soon felt, did not really welcome us children. It was said that he could neither read nor write, and that when the service-car driver threw him the morning paper, he looked at it assiduously, even though it was usually upside-down! That, I think, was probably an exaggeration fostered by the service-car drivers to amuse their passengers on the tedious journey. The bachelor was a good neighbour, but certainly he kept to himself, seeming to be interested in little but his stock.

We children learnt not to go near his dwelling as he stood outside it fixing us with a silent stare if we approached. He and Father got on well, however, and held long doleful conversations about stock prices and rates. His home was a rough whare made of pit-sawn timber and papered inside with the picture section of the *Auckland Weekly News*. It was said that he was fairly well off and was sent an annuity from an estate in England. He was a stoutish man. My people sensed that he had had an unhappy history and perhaps was not the formidable character he seemed. He was a shrewd man with money and during the worst of the slump when he, like everyone else, found prices for his wool abysmally low, decided to store it. He could apparently afford to do so, and for four years his woolshed was piled high with bales of wool. Some were even pushed into his whare, which gave it a rich aroma. He sold the wool when prices came right, to great advantage.

Strange tales were told of the bachelor. One day, his dwelling caught fire. A neighbour happened to ride by and found him calmly contemplating the fire as it burned. The neighbour was puzzled and leapt off his horse shouting, 'Come on, man, let's save some of your things.' The bachelor shook his head and said slowly, 'I wouldn't go near it, if I were you. There's a keg of gunpowder inside.' There was great speculation after that. It was said, of course, that it was probably an 'insurance job'. After the fire he raked out from the ashes, the iron work of saddles, pack saddles and harness. He'd recently bought up a quantity of these from neighbours. Then he proceeded to build a much more comfortable, three-roomed whare of milled timber brought in from Gisborne.

The bachelor often told, with relish, of the visit of a 'swagger' who passed frequently through the Gorge. (He appeared to resent tramps greatly and all-in-all he certainly had the reputation for having little of the milk of human kindness in his character.) He asked the man in, and while the kettle was boiling, started on him.

'Does any of your relations know you're in the Gorge?'

'No. Damn relations don't bother me now.'

'Does anyone expect you at Gisborne?'

'No. I'm on me own, like.'

The bachelor then picked up a meat cleaver.

'If I cut off your bloody head, tie your heels together behind the old mare and drag you up the valley and dump you, nobody will miss you!'

The bachelor's story was that he then reached across the stove for the kettle, to make the man a cup of tea. 'But when I turned around, the impatient beggar had left,' he would conclude dryly.

Managing a farm nearby was a Londoner of Cockney descent, whose ruling passion was cricket. He was shrewd, kind-hearted, and always cheerful. His enthusiasm for cricket infected the people of Matawai, especially the schoolboys. In weekends he was to be found in the school grounds, ever hopeful that enough adults and children would turn up to make a match. When they did, he was everywhere at once, yelling encouragement, batting wildly and running up the makeshift pitch, a mown strip of the school rugby field, as fast as his legs would carry him. Or he would catch a short one, arms flailing as he lost his balance.

The Londoner was regarded by all as a 'decent little chap' and it was the ambition of the older boys (and some of the men) to 'bowl him out for a duck egg'. He turned up in his cricket whites as dapper as if he was to play in an English county match, and this was a bit much for pioneering Matawai.

Further down the Gorge, another neighbour lived on a difficult section across the river. Like most people, he was getting deeply into debt. A stock agent from his stock and station firm was sent out from Opotiki to count his sheep in order to make an inventory of his assets. The neighbour and his teenage sons mustered the first valley and the sheep were carefully counted. The father then said to the stock agent, who was young and naive, 'We'll have some lunch now, and then you might like to try your hand with me at a trout. There's usually one in the pool there below the house. I'll lend you a rod.' After a pleasant hour and a half, the agent was taken to the next set of yards where more sheep were counted. They were the same mob, driven over the hill by the sons of the house while lunch and the fishing were in progress. Eventually the firm could be held off no longer, even by such survival tactics. The stock was quietly sold off, and the family disappeared, leaving an abandoned farm.

A certain Mr S of Wairata was lent money by a government

department to cut bush, sow seed and put up fences on his section. When all this was carried out, he applied for more money to buy stock. But his request was refused, point-blank; government credit had tightened up, and in the eyes of officialdom he'd already had more than his share of the limited loan money available.

The Prime Minister, Mr Coates, paid a short visit to Opotiki some time later in response to urgent appeals from the Opotiki district settlers to survey their plight. They hoped that they might be given some relief on the interest owing on their mortgages. A deputation lunched in Opotiki's Masonic Hotel with the Prime Minister.

'Mr Coates, you must get some odd requests at times,' said one settler, making conversation.

The Prime Minister pulled a letter from his pocket, and said, 'Yes, I do. Listen to this.'

The letter he read was the one Mr S had written.

Mr S, who was present, walked over to the Prime Minister and, white-faced, swore at him in vivid language before striding out of the room.

Government departments in the nineteen thirties were slow to understand the problems of bush farming. And soldier settlers were a political minority.

Poverty and hardship bred a desperate sort of courage in places like the Waioeka. Originally, there had been twenty-six families settled along the Gorge, after World War I, but one by one they left as times became harder. They were kindly hard-working people and it must have been heart-breaking for them to abandon their earlier hopes of building farms. Their children mostly turned out to be sturdy and reliable folk, who eventually did well in the wider world. One such stalwart family, whose mother had kept the Wairata school going by teaching there, produced fine teachers, one of whom became a university lecturer. Gibson's Bridge is named after them.

Then there was the Irish roadman, kind-hearted to a degree, married to a quiet Maori woman. There were annual additions to this family, each one an interesting event to us children. Mother was usually called in to help and thought the mother was very brave. When I came to produce my own babies, there was quite a

lot I had to unlearn, via the writings of such an enlightened gynae-
cologist as Dr Grantly Dick Read. The father in this family also
consoled himself with 'John Barleycorn'. Their large brood was to
be a trump card in the paper war soon to be waged by Mother and
and Father to obtain a school bus to Matawai. As there were now
ten children 'over the Hill', they really had a case. Eventually, it
was recognized by the department. Had it not been, my family
would have moved out then and there, I think, so highly did they
place the necessity of a good education.

The Gorge, with its sprinkling of deserted farmhouses standing
in high fern, was and is regarded as an eerie place by outsiders.
Legends have grown up about it. Of course, there was the one
about Te Kooti. It was said that when his forces were overcome at
the mouth of the Gorge, Te Kooti had to flee further into the
interior of the Ureweras. The trenches from the battle are still to
be seen, notching the high ferny ridges guarding the entrance from
Opotiki. Te Kooti, a religious mystic, then placed a curse upon the
Gorge and all who inhabited it. Sometimes, I think, our elders
thought of this story with secret apprehension in moments of
bitterness and trouble. The Scots have respect for such matters.

There was another legend about a nearby valley. It was said that
in the moonlight, at dead of night, a ghostly legion of soldiers
marched down its slopes to band music and that also, at times, the
sounds of galloping horses were to be heard there. I suppose I was
an impressionable child, but one night, sleeping on a porch, I
awoke to brilliant moonlight. I was sure that the valley was echoing
and ringing to the regular thud of horses' hooves. But though the
clear light of waking reason told me it must have been a dream,
Mother looked at me wonderingly for a second, before she firmly
pooh-poohed the incident.

Father once had a frightening experience. He was walking down
the steep dark valley of the soldiers legend at dusk, and suddenly
there came wafting up the creek in the clear air, the most sinister
noises – a heavy stamping and banging, and overall a ringing metal-
lic sound. In telling us the story, he admitted to being frightened
and more than a little puzzled. The dogs suddenly stopped in their
tracks, howled woefully, and raised stiff hackles. But father
tramped on towards whatever-it-was. Nearing the road, the noises

became louder and there, in a hollow, was the deserted fencer's hut, rocking and vibrating with noise from its sheet iron sides. By now father could hear cattle bellowing. He wrenched open the door, and six emaciated steers rushed past him in the twilight, straight towards the creek. They had sheltered in the hut in a storm, and had become firmly shut in, the door having latched from the inside.

On some nights, when a small unfriendly moon rode high and remote behind dark ragged clouds and a harsh restless wind scoured the slopes and valleys, the atmosphere of the Gorge oppressed us children. How different it was in the bright confident sunshine of daytime! We always felt that the freight-car drivers were its real heroes, driving through its long isolated tortuous reaches at dead of night, in all weathers. We often awoke from sleep, snugly tucked in our beds, to hear the heavy truck grinding up the Hill, after stopping to collect our cream cans. One driver at least, went to sleep at the wheel, and never returned to his family.

13

Better Times

Towards the late nineteen thirties, our life as a family seemed to reach a kind of equilbrium and a pleasant maturity. The worst strains of the depression were behind us, and New Zealand entered a period of moderate prosperity as prices for our primary products on the overseas market steadily improved. The prevailing mood was one of temperate optimism.

On the farm, we continued our efforts with the cows, and the selling of eggs, and occasionally the hard-won potato or swede crop yielded some extra bags for sale. We had long learned to dread stock sale days, but now Father would come home from a sale at Matawai, or Opotiki, whence the sheep had been slowly driven by one of Father's drover friends, well pleased with the price for his wethers. They did well on the Gorge country, in spite of its steepness.

One day Father returned from Gisborne, in the late afternoon, driving a new car. Actually it was second-hand, but it had been well cared for. It was a large Chrysler, resplendent in maroon paint and immaculately chromed about the bumpers and headlamps. Our first glimpse of it, glancing through the poplar grove by the woolshed, its chrome catching the sunlight brilliantly, thrilled us immeasurably, and we could not believe it was really ours. The comfort and convenience of a reliable car, large enough to carry all the family, was indeed an asset. The road was steadily improving as the open fords were bridged, and so visits were made to other branches of the family to renew the links between us. We sometimes arrived unexpectedly, but we always took a contribution of food with us. Fresh butter, eggs and a joint of meat were stowed away in the capacious boot, along with our individual small suitcases, which provided us with great excitement in their packing. We were always welcomed with great hospitality by the flats relatives at

'Toroa' or at 'Waiohika', whose way of life was more formal. In turn they, together with some of their town friends, enjoyed fishing and hunting weekends, and picnics in the Gorge with us.

Another new amenity was a radio, an 'all-waves' one, which, marvel of marvels, enabled us to hear German or Japanese people speaking. At first we sat up until signing-off time, night after night, and Uncle Scrim of the 'Friendly Road' programme was our favourite. Grandma regarded the radio as a mixed blessing, and worried about its introducing the evils of the world into our home, and their effect upon our developing minds. But when she was able to hear one of her respected ministers preach from a city cathedral, she began to evaluate the new medium more favourably.

The aunts always arrived for the holidays and many vigorous political discussions took place during substantial morning teas, when the family gathered on one of the open porches. The aunts helped Mother refurbish her sitting-room, sewing curtains in cheerful floral linens, and embroidering new runners for the shelves and sideboard. A large carpet square, in Mother's favourite gold and tawny colours, was added. When the table was set for dinner with white roses in the mahogany and silver biscuit barrel for a centre-piece, the room had its own charm in the soft light of the Aladdin lamp, with the light of the fire glowing mellowly upon the oiled wood fireplace surround. The kitchen equipment was overhauled, and a new and gleaming enamelled woodstove, replacing the old black one, was bought, together with a white porcelain bath and basin for the bathroom. The old galvanized iron bath-tub, with its ornate claw feet, had served for many years and had been leaking badly. Mother's joy in all these improvements was unbounded and richly deserved. She was ever a home-maker.

Grandmother was becoming more frail, and at about this time a shadow fell upon our happiness, as she was overtaken by serious illness. After spending some time in hospital, which she hated as it meant separation from the family, she returned home, but her illness was little improved. It was kept from us children as much as possible. We had missed her sadly, and in Cook Hospital in Gisborne she had often looked longingly towards her beloved hills, visible in the far distance. It was decided that another room should be added to the house, so that she could be close to the family. This was soon planned and built. It was spacious and airy, with two large double windows and its own big fireplace. It was connected with the house kitchen by its own little porch. All the family contributed to the considerable expense of this addition. On one of his Opotiki trips, Father had to choose wallpaper for it, unaided by feminine help. Mother had her misgivings about this, and when he arrived with the mysterious bundle of white rolls, he placed them ceremoniously upon the kitchen table, and put his hat on top playfully, saying, 'Well, here you are, you had better all have a say and get it over!' We girls were beginning to be quite vocal in our opinions, too. But when one sample was unrolled and held up, and we admired the dainty climbing rose pattern on a cream ground, it was generally conceded that for a man he had done very well. Grandmother had to have the best, we all felt.

Grandmother must have felt it sorely, having to give up her independence and her cottage, but she never complained. The new room contained recessed shelves for her books, and there was room for her beloved piano. Here the aunts sometimes played to her: Grieg, whose music of the mountains she loved, or Mendelssohn. Little by little, she had to spend more time in bed. But after school we always visited her in her room, to be read to, or to read to her from our latest School Journals. And she insisted that, as the eldest, I should be taught music. I had now become quite proficient at picking out tunes by ear, on which practice Grandmother rather frowned. I was sent by service-car to Matawai, where a young music teacher from a cultured family of friends, came to teach music on Saturday afternoons to a group of pupils. I greatly admired her, and looked forward to the weekly lesson. It meant that I had to stay the night and return to the Gorge next day, and Sister Pritchard, who had an ever-generous interest in young people, offered to have me stay. She was later awarded the O.B.E. for her service to the hill country people.

And so I practised in Grandma's room under her sensitive ear. I was never allowed to strum or slur the notes. I progressed well, and was soon able to read music and play such well chosen pieces as McDowell's 'To a Wild Rose', which I loved. Later I was able to sit and pass some music examinations. The piano was to be my consolation in the bad patches of life, as I'm sure it was Grandmother's.

And now a passion for reading seized us, especially me. I devoured everything of the printed word which came into the house, and inevitably was teased by all the family and called 'the bookworm'. While absorbed in a book, I lived and felt it, becoming fairly oblivious to everything around me. The big old chestnut tree at the bottom of the garden, overlooking the creek, had an inviting fork high in its hospitable mantle of branches, and this became my daytime retreat in the hours when I was free from school or chores. Sometimes, I am sorry to say, they called me in vain. At night, after bedtime, I would re-light the candle, and read surreptitiously, my fingers chilled to the marrow, until it grew really late and I collected a scolding if discovered by the concerned adults. I read on — the *Weekly News* (we had always loved 'The Gum Nut Babies' series when younger), the local *Herald*, the newspaper *Truth* (which Father often bought), as well as most of Dickens, *Tom Brown's Schooldays*, *Little Women*, also Emily and Charlotte Bronte, Jane Austen, Hardy, Conrad, Rider Haggard, Maning's *Old New Zealand*, *Kimble Bent*, and stories of the Maori Wars, Grandmother's copy of *Tales of the Borders* by Scott — my taste was all encompassing. To me, each reading experience represented part of the world beyond the encircling hills, which I was determined to penetrate, if at this stage only via the printed word.

14

Grandmother

Throughout her long, full, and useful life, lived for the most part in the mountains, Grandmother held an unshakeable belief in Providence. In moments of stress she always referred to it. The idea contained her belief in a moral Power behind the visible universe, and she found the concept well expressed by the psalmists of the Old Testament. Her favourite was, of course, the well loved Twenty-Third Psalm.

And now she herself was about to enter the 'Valley of the Shadow of Death'. Her life was quietly drawing to its close, and her physical world was bounded by her room and her bed. One by one the aunts, even her married daughters, returned to the farm to stay and care for her as she became increasingly weak and helpless. Two of the aunts were nurses, and blessedly they were able to give her some relief from pain as the illness progressed. But her mind never faltered. She was keenly concerned with and interested in the family and farm until the last, and her piercing blue eyes always lit up whenever she saw us children. We sensed the shadow, and were at first very disturbed and rebellious that such things should be. Even a vague longing for her release stirred in us. Mother sensed our suffering and helped us to this acceptance as well as she could.

One lovely night in late spring, when all the aunts were gathered at the homestead, and they sat talking quietly around the fireplace in Grandmother's room, we knew that the end was near. By morning she lay peacefully at rest, her strong features softened in death. We were allowed to tip-toe into her room to pay our last respects.

As the full realization of our loss set in, the world seemed to spin dizzily. Later on, a black hearse came slowly down the Hill to the homestead, and the long polished wood coffin was sorrowfully carried out by Father and Cousin Stewart. This moment was too much for us, and we hid in the bamboo, squeezed close together, crying the silent bitter tears of childhood. For us the pure rainbow colours of life, perceived only by children, were suddenly blurred and faded.

We were spared the funeral. Before the hearse departed, Mother and the aunts heaped the casket with masses of early roses picked from the garden. They, too, cried quietly, and spoke little as they picked the flowers together. Grandmother's silent and empty room with her familiar bow-fronted dresser and oval mirror still in their place, and the empty bed, were painfully avoided by us for many months.

Grandmother's passing had taken place in her beloved mountains and she was surrounded by those dearest to her. In this thought we all eventually took some comfort. But for us elder children, childhood's rainbow had vanished, never to return.

15

Beyond the Gorge

Now we were growing up fast. For our parents the troubling thought of our secondary schooling was ever present. Those pupils who passed the final exams from primary school with credit, were eligible to receive a boarding bursary to attend secondary school. But at present we were receiving only three hours of schooling a day, and so the adults feared we might not reach the required standard after all. The cost of boarding Larry and me at 'The Rectory' and 'Ayton House' (the secondary school boarding establishments in Gisborne), even with bursary, together with the cost of our uniforms (which were very formal), was almost beyond the slender resources of a hill country farm. And there were now ten children from the Gorge, an embarrassing number for the service-car drivers to stow. They were still taking us to Wairata School, but our parents felt that the generosity of the service-car company as well as the drivers was really being imposed upon.

Mother and Father therefore decided to open determined negotiations with the Education Board for a school bus. The distance to each of the nearest schools was sixteen kilometres, but Matawai supported a two teacher school, and had shopping and social amenities, and so they felt that it would offer more in the way of social experience for us. After a lengthy correspondence, representatives of the Education Board and of the Department of Education in Wellington, the local Member of Parliament, and the Minister of Education met the parents concerned at a function held at Matawai School. Mr Peter Fraser, who was the Minister of Education and a fatherly figure, cheerfully signed autograph books for us children. Better still, he granted the school bus, after hearing of the educational predicament of the Waioeka and other settlers. An enterprising young storekeeper from Matawai took the conveyance contract and provided the bus and a store delivery service. The bus was quite adequate according to the standards of the day, and was a blessing for those children along the route near Matawai who had formerly walked to school. Two long padded bench-type seats were mounted lengthways on a truck deck and the whole was covered with a canvas hood and closed in at the back where we mounted steps and entered through a little door. The main factor in the success of the bus was the skill and reliability of the young driver, and my parents were very comforted by this, as the road over the Hill provided no easy driving. The surface was very slippery in frost or snow, and the grades were still one in three in many places.

On the many frosty mornings, we wrapped up in rugs, took hot water bottles, and sang all the way to school to keep warm. On the steep grades the children nearest the cab had to keep a tight hold of the seatbacks, or be shot downwards along the narrow bench to lean heavily upon their neighbours, who protested and elbow jolted them. Larry and I, as seniors, had to keep the peace but we were mostly a happy group, and chattered and sang together. The bus trip was still the event of the day for many of us.

Thus a whole new section of the world beyond the Gorge opened up for us. Matawai was still the centre of the hill country community, where farming (mostly of sheep but there were some fine dairy herds) and sawmilling were carried on. It had small shops and enough business concerns to make the community fairly independent of the larger centres, yet as everyone knew everybody else, it was somewhat like a large family. At first we had to go through the business of settling in to a new school again. But this time, as we were older, it did not take very long. Our teacher 'E.E.' was to have a lasting influence upon our outlook and development. He was a widely cultured man of strong personality, who demanded and got high standards of work from most of us. He had the art of drawing forth our best efforts, in schoolwork, art, or sport. To him we were individual and unique personalities, and he seemed shrewdly able to judge our capabilities, simply refusing to accept second-best from anyone. He was a strict disciplinarian. He realized and sympathized with my struggle to relate to the wider world. 'There is mere existence', he would tell us, 'and there is the richness of true living and awareness.' He opened many doors for us.

He had travelled Europe widely, riding on the new autobahns in

Germany, staying along the Mediterranean coast, and visiting much of Britain, telling us especially of Oxford and Cambridge. And so he gave us vital glimpses of the world. We were fortunate indeed to come in contact with such a teacher. He had both the highest ideals of teaching, and a driving ambition to realize some of them with even such unpromising material as we must have seemed. Books, music, and art were his spiritual life-blood, and he encouraged my growing passion for them. He made me feel that nothing could stop personal development if one had the desire to work for it.

The local postmaster was also a well educated man, who introduced me to Van Loon's *Story of Mankind*, which helped to fill some of the abysmal gaps in my knowledge of elementary history and geography. Our teacher continued to take the greatest interest in this family from the Gorge, and sometimes spent weekends with my parents when they all talked far into the night. He confided to Mother that he had not been overjoyed at the prospect of ten 'bush children' being suddenly added to the school, and was delighted to find that we were an unexpected asset. But he never overcame Mother's prejudice, born of her day and age, against university education for women. ('Bluestockings — and unhappy old maids' was the ubiquitous summary amongst farming people of the time, I am sorry to say.) No, not for one of *her* daughters - it might prejudice my chances of marriage. 'Drinking and study spoil girls!' she said. Mother really believed this.

They were materially progressive years for the hill country communities, those golden years just before World War II. Again, if there was tension in the adult world because of the approaching storm, we children were unaware of it. All the hill country schools gathered for sports days to compete in friendly rivalry, which raised a din of barracking to the very skies. We became part of a team, a new experience for us, and we were able to be flippant or disapproving about differences in dress or mannerism met with in those comprising the other teams. In the mutual consumption of lavish afternoon teas, including sponge cakes with whipped cream, shortbread, Louise cakes, such as only hill country mothers could produce, casual friendships sprang up. Such social progress was always noticed and valued by our teacher. We often travelled to neighbouring schools by train, which added to the bliss of the day. We sang to the clackety-clack of wheels on rails, now rapid, now slowing to a walking pace on the steep grades, the small valiant 'K' class locomotive puffing and heaving at the task. Some hardy souls stood on the platform outside the carriage while the train went through a tunnel, for which they were strapped next morning if caught, which was a sad anticlimax to all the excitement. One boy spread-eagled himself on the roof of a carriage, while the train travelled through a tunnel. He survived this and a severe strapping when caught. He had almost choked to death with the smoke but was a hero, of course, in the eyes of some of the other boys.

Numbers in the upper school did not provide two football teams. So that the boys could have match practice, we girls were required to play too and thoroughly enjoyed a vigorous game of rugby in the clear frosty blueness of a Matawai morning with the sun glinting coldly but promisingly on the distinctive peaks visible from the playground. Sometimes there were bruises, bleeding noses, and brief tears. E.E. was a strict referee and made no concessions on account of our sex.

School fancy dress balls were held in the ancient village hall, its wide planked wooden floor thumping thrillingly to the strains of 'The Sultan's Grand March', played on the piano by a local lass, the rhythm emphasized by a hundred sturdy legs. And the antics of a 'cow' of brown burlap with black and white rolling eyes and a set of real Hereford horns, with a slightly bashful milkmaid, costumed in English style, following it uncertainly in the procession, brought hysterical appreciation from the onlookers, including our erstwhile strict teacher. The cow's grotesque and sudden lurching movements, and the at times plaintive and argumentative sounds issuing from the region of its middle, were irresistible. Mother had spent hours making that cow for Larry and a mate to dress up in, while Gael was the timid milkmaid. I preferred to go as 'Spring' all decked out in lemon silk and carrying a posy of deep blue grape hyacinths.

After the school dancing the grown-ups had their turn, and there was a rush across the floor for partners for the First Waltz. At the doorway the young male contingent of the district gathered, bashfully or boldly, and the uncertain ones were left standing. It was always our secret hope, in Standard Six, that we would be asked to dance by the young gallants from the farms. And of course we were, especially if dressed as 'Spring'. Piano-accordion music made the old walls resound and the smoky lanterns overhead swing gently. Sometimes the dancing was accompanied by violin and piano, all the players being local musicians. Families gathered with families for the new Palais Glide, while the Military Two-Step left everyone quite breathless, such was the pace and spirit of the music. We loved it all and too soon it was time to pile into the car, and drive homewards over the winding hill road in the heavy frost, which periodically had to be cleared from the windscreen. Once we took Horace, our tiny dark brown reptilian-looking pet opossum, in a basket, as we were afraid the cats might be tempted to sample him in our absence. Of course, he was shown to the curious, at which we were rewarded by shrieks and laughter. The Gorge children certainly had some strange ways, but on the whole we were well tolerated. On our part we began to feel hardy and independent.

There were concerts, where the local village prima donna, decked in a frothy pink tulle dress and a diamanté necklace, wistfully sang the latest sentimental ballad and received prolonged applause, whistling, and stamping, at which she managed to look slightly disdainful. We thought her terribly courageous and she probably was. The school choir then had to line up with our teacher's stern eye upon us, and after much scuffling and pushing, especially amid the back rows where the boys were, we settled down to produce a quite impressive flow of sound, for we really loved singing. The anaesthetizing effect of facing the footlights and the audience lasted until the concluding verse, and we never did our teacher justice by singing as we could have.

E.E., our teacher, helped us to develop our art work, especially the making of posters. In his concentration upon drawing forth creative expression, he must have been well ahead of his time. I remember his interest in a dramatic if not lurid picture I produced of the Gorge sun setting behind the rugged silhouette of purple-black hills. To me, of course, it was a kind of private symbol. The training we received in design and formal poster-type lettering was to be an asset over the years, as was his meticulous insistence upon the learning of English grammar in our compositions. We absorbed much about farming and agriculture, and the place it occupied in the country's economy. A study of local industry, soils, and topography was made. Collections of native flora were pressed and named and the study of native birds was encouraged. (In the 'Raysburn' kitchen, there had hung since our earliest years a framed *Weekly News* colour supplement depicting New Zealand birds and we had identified many of them in the surrounding bush.) Granite-like rocks of the Gorge country with their veins of a white crystalline substance fascinated us. On our expeditions to the bush we felt the extreme joy of discovering what might be a new or rare plant, and then looking up its botanical name in sources provided by E.E. The dainty Prince of Wales plumed fern was always a treasure to us. Also we learned to distinguish the juvenile forms of some plants such as the lancewood, and marvelled that their appearance was to be so changed as they matured. Somehow I dimly grasped that the 'ugly duckling' theme could apply equally to animals, plants and, most importantly, humans. We also learned to swim the crawl stroke properly, going daily down the dusty road in a long crocodile to the silvery coolness of the local river, which was not far from the school. Life had become full and satisfying.

We or I, at least, loved learning with a rare passion and E.E. was a compelling mentor. From him and from our former teachers at Wairata we had caught the personal boon (or curse) of an insatiable curiosity about everything, which, of course, is a prerequisite to most achievement.

Epilogue

Time moved me on, first to the local town for boarding school and secondary education. Here I attained the coveted matriculation in three short years. And then into a city and the emotional maelstrom of a city in wartime – I trained for teaching, and managed to attend university as a part-time student. I sat in the dreary wartime trams and looked at the dreary faces of the people opposite. For me, they were Blake's faces, from his 'London' with 'marks of weakness, marks of woe'. Like Grandmother, I was an expatriate and knew it.

At the first opportunity I returned to the mountains as a sole-charge teacher. Later (as Mother had probably foreseen), I married a farming man. Together we faced in our own time the challenge of an undeveloped farm in the backblocks. And later we bought another smaller farm nearer Gisborne, to winter some of the high-country stock in the foothills.

In looking back from adulthood it seems to me that we were indeed fortunate in our childhood. We were free, to a more than usual degree, to develop naturally. Our lives contained the optimum of the beauty, harmony, and innocence of a young childhood left to itself as much as possible, and lived continuously in contact with natural elements. Such experiences as we had in developing the senses, contribute to later intellect. Mother held these views, valuing highly generosity, warmth, and spontaneity in human relationships. On the other hand, Grandmother and Father evidently held the view that character was to be built by elders, little by little and at times painfully. We were never conscious as children of this dichotomy, and of the probable conflicts which took place. And as the intrusion of the world was inevitable as we emerged beyond the hills, Grandmother's views were perhaps a necessary preparation for the harder realities of adulthood. Between them our adults had represented to us the main philosophical views of life prevalent in European culture in the time of their childhood.

The adults appeared to share the humanitarian view that what we are as individuals is more important than class or possessions. Their courage in the face of the giants 'Want' and 'Despair' was, and is, a lasting example to all of us. So, too, was their kindness and concern at the suffering of any living thing. The qualities of courage and compassion were possessed by them in no small measure, I think.

Our individualism was fostered and yet we learned to cooperate as a group. There was abundant challenge in our environment to fire our youthful imaginations and give us the joy of achievement. But of course a childhood spent in isolation from the mainstream of the world was also at times a very real handicap in adult life.

Inevitably the close-knit childhood group scattered widely in adulthood. From it there emerged a variety of personalities, all with useful occupations. There are two educators, one of whom has inspired and organized a holiday camp extending throughout a province for schoolchildren, in which parents participate to give their children the invaluable experience of living and learning within an area of natural bush-clad New Zealand. Another has contributed by means of a Doctorate of Philosophy, in a quiet but brilliant way, to understanding between the races. There are two teachers, one of whom was to travel widely overseas and the other to help in the field of pre-school education in a rural area, and one nurse, who practised her profession overseas as well as serving the rural areas. In addition, we have several knowledgeable farmers, all of whom are experienced deerstalkers and good marksmen, and (may I add in all modesty) a scribe — the natural metamorphosis of a bookworm! All have families who were given bush experience as often as possible, as were the children of our friends.

One of these friends was to be a city doctor, who gave immeasurable help and support to my husband Keith and me in the years of isolation and struggle to establish our own farm. When I first met Dr B. as a patient, I was about to produce my first child and betook myself to him, reluctantly, for gynaecological advice. I liked him instantly. During that first interview (in which I was not my most enthusiastic self!) something made him look at me with a direct

gaze and say 'You are fey!' I returned flippantly, trying to be cheerful, 'Yes. I was born beneath a rainbow!'

'What *do* you mean?' said he, intrigued.

'Well, I'll write a book about it some day, when I've got time —
maybe in another thirty years or so . . .'

And the Gorge?

My people left 'Raysburn' in the early nineteen forties to manage
a property belonging to Mother's family and to release an uncle for
active service in World War II. Then they acquired a twenty-nine
hectare (seventy acre) farm on the plain, but continued to stock
'Raysburn' with sheep as a necessary addition to their limited
income.

Except for the descendants of two families settled on the slightly
easier terrain of the Wairata Valley, and an elderly childless couple
who hung on in the lower Gorge, all of the original settlers had
gone, their land abandoned. All over the central and coastal North
Island region, land which had been settled by soldiers returned
from World War I under government schemes, was similarly abandoned, left to revert to fern. These settlers and their families had
fought a courageous but heart-breaking battle with the odds
stacked against them from the beginning of their tenure. The col-
lapse of prices for their only products, meat and wool, in overseas
markets in the nineteen thirties was the final blow to the hopes of
thousands of farming people.

In the Gorge, the farms which survived are now benefitting from
the new technology of aerial top-dressing, modern mechanization,
a more sympathetic government attitude to farming, and more
realistic rentals. The easier parts of 'Raysburn' are still farmed as
my parents farmed it, by some of the family as a run-off for the flats
property. This land, too, is being developed with modern technology.

The modern Waioeka Gorge route was officially opened on a
misty December day in 1962, by Mr W.S. Goosman, then Minister
of Works. At the centre of the ceremony was the unveiling of a
large slab of natural Gorge stone, carrying a tablet engraved with
the names of those who lost their lives in the building of the road.
Tributes were paid to the engineers and workmen who laboured in

the forties and fifties to upgrade the road from a one-way metalled track to a six metre sealed highway. One speaker referred to 'this fine and beautiful road, carved out of impossibility.'

My parents were official guests, and some of the family (including myself), were present. For my Father this was an hour of fulfilment. In addition to his efforts in the earlier years to see the road established, he had served on the National Roads Board, to help represent Gisborne's interests in the completion of the northern outlet.

The thoughts of all were long, long thoughts. We remembered the men, many of them Maori, who drove the heavy earth-moving machinery along the towering rock faces with consummate skill. Maori Bluff was forty-nine metres high. These road faces were cut down from the top with bulldozers, layer by layer, while the spoil tumbled into the river, diverting it by some twelve metres in places with tonnes and tonnes of rock and shale. As the Gorge echoed to the roar of the machines, vibrations caused slips. One of these buried a workman up to his neck, but left him unhurt. Often massive trees fell from the tops as a whole section of bush gave way.

Sometimes a great bulldozer would somersault off the edge as the rock beneath changed to shale. Cool-headed, the drivers usually managed to jump clear. But one who did not, arrived, miraculously still in his seat, upon the river bed, a dazed grin on his face while his mates roared with laughter in relief.

We thought of the man who lost his arm in the metal crusher, who coolly walked down its ladder, holding his shoulder and travelled forty-eight kilometres to hospital in a truck cab with an occasional quick grin to his mates.

Such was the spirit of these men. We thought of how they had worked cheerfully month by month in pouring rain, or in scorching heat, or waist-deep in the icy winter waters of the river. The Gorge has always demanded courage and a sense of humour. Without these qualities humans would not survive living and working there.

This concentrated work had taken eleven years and cost $2.5 million, so the opening was indeed a day of achievement.

But the Gorge was not yet tamed. Perhaps Tawhiri Matea, the Maori god of storms, was angry. Or the spirits of the ancient people buried here, restless. Fifteen months after the opening ceremony, a huge flood arose and the river roared and rushed madly, nine metres above its normal level, tearing at the road until it was eroded in many places, right back to its white centre line. Months more of patient work and $300,000 went into repairing it. In February 1967, another huge flood occurred. This time it cost $730,000 to put the road to rights. But now it seems, the scars have healed, and the sides of the Gorge have consolidated, though some maintenance is still necessary.

Perhaps the ancients sleep, assuaged at last.

The beauty of the Gorge is now accessible to all. Nowadays I pass through or visit it frequently. In high spring at full midday, the sun is brilliant and the air has a soft transparent clarity. Sunlight dances on the rapids and flecks the smooth surface of the emerald green deep water. As I travel the swinging curves of bitumen, the hills seem to fold in closely and the blue ranges overlap in the distance. Then the hills open to reveal a vision of wide sky and deep-piled clouds. I feel gloriously alive here. It's part of me now, this Gorge, ever lovely, ever beguiling. For in growing up and coming to awareness here, the memories of rain, sun and wind on its forested slopes, of the sound of running water on stones, of the light on the hills against the sky, of the sights and smells of the bush, became forever woven into my mind and remain fresh, even after fifty years. I know, too, that my grandparents and parents developed a spiritual feeling about this place and I believe they are somehow still part of it. There is great peace in the thought.

And the coming generations?

They have access to a vast wilderness now known as the Waioeka Gorge National Reserve, which will enhance their lives and be a treasured area for their recreation and renewal. Along the old bridle-tracks up the side valleys, made by the early settlers, walking-tracks are being developed. Tucked unobtrusively into the bush on the flats, caravan and camping sites are being established. There are the Gorge mountains, such as Maungawhiorangi, to climb. From there you can see the sun rising gloriously over the eastern mountains and the sea. There are the myriad small streams and the larger rivers in which to fish for a rainbow trout, or see a rare blue mountain duck fly up a lonely valley.

The highest point of the road over the Raukumaras, is now officially named 'Trafford's Hill' after my family. My son, and now my nephews and grandsons, learnt the ancient arts of the bushman and the huntsman on 'Raysburn'. Those well loved 600 hectares, still our family home, are visited and enjoyed regularly. And we share the old, old traditions of Gorge hospitality with others who love the bush.

*The New Women's Press was founded in 1982 to publish books by, for,
and about women.*

   Titles already published are:
Healthy Women: A Self-Help Guide to Good Health *by Sarah
Calvert*
Self Defence for Women *by Sue Lytollis*
New Zealand Herstory — *an annual biographical diary recording the lives
and achievements of New Zealand women*

   *For information about forthcoming titles, write to: New Women's Press,
P.O. Box 47-339, Auckland.*